World War I
Biographies

World War I
Biographies

Tom Pendergast
and Sara Pendergast

Christine Slovey, Editor

GALE GROUP
™
THOMSON LEARNING

Detroit • New York • San Diego • San Francisco
Boston • New Haven, Conn. • Waterville, Maine
London • Munich

World War I: Biographies

Tom Pendergast and Sara Pendergast

Staff

Christine Slovey, *U•X•L Senior Editor*
Julie L. Carnagie, *U•X•L Contributing Editor*
Carol DeKane Nagel, *U•X•L Managing Editor*
Tom Romig, *U•X•L Publisher*

Pamela A.E. Galbreath, *Senior Art Director (Page design)*
Jennifer Wahi, *Art Director (Cover design)*

Shalice Shah-Caldwell, *Permissions Associate (Images)*
Robyn Young, *Imaging and Multimedia Content Editor*
Pamela A. Reed, *Imaging Coordinator*
Robert Duncan, *Imaging Specialist*

Rita Wimberly, *Senior Buyer*
Evi Seoud, *Assistant Manager, Composition Purchasing and Electronic Prepress*

Linda Mahoney, LM Design, *Typesetting*

Cover Photos: Woodrow Wilson and Manfred von Richthofen reproduced by permission of AP/Wide World Photos, Inc.

Library of Congress Cataloging-in-Publication Data

Pendergast, Tom.
World War I biographies / Tom Pendergast, Sara Pendergast
    p.cm.
   Includes bibliographical references and index.
   Summary: A collection of thirty biographies of world figures who played important roles in World War I, including Mata Hari, T.E. Lawrence, and Alvin C. York.
  ISBN 0-7876-5477-9
   1. World War, 1914-1918—Biography—Dictionaries—Juvenile literature. [1. World War, 1914-1918—Biography. 2. Soldiers.] I. Title: World War One biographies. II. Title: World War 1 biographies. III. Pendergast, Sara. IV. Title.

D522.7 .P37 2001
940.3'092'2--dc21
                                          2001053162

Contents

Edith Cavell. *Reproduced by permission of Archive Photos, Inc.*

Antigas precaution sign.
Reproduced by permission of Hulton Getty/Archive Photos, Inc.

Reader's Guide

World War I was truly one of the most tragic events of the twentieth century. The war began over a terrorist act in the provinces of the fading Austro-Hungarian Empire and could have been avoided if Germany, Russia, and France hadn't felt compelled to obey secret treaties they had signed years before. Those secret treaties turned a small conflict into one that involved every major country in Europe and eventually many other nations from around the world. In the course of just over four years of war, nearly ten million soldiers and civilians lost their lives; billions of dollars were spent on killing machines—guns, tanks, submarines—and the economies of most of the warring countries were severely disrupted; and two great empires—the Austro-Hungarian Empire and the Ottoman Empire—collapsed in defeat.

At the end of this terrible conflict, little had changed. Ethnic conflicts in the Balkan region continued to pit neighbor against neighbor. Attempts to create an international organization that would ensure world peace collapsed when the United States withdrew its support. Germany, though defeated, remained at odds with its rivals, France and England,

and military leaders within Germany longed to avenge their defeat. Within twenty years of the end of World War I, these simmering tensions sparked another war, World War II, which returned death and destruction to the continent of Europe and to battlefields all over the world.

World War I: Biographies contains essays on twenty-eight people who were involved in the war. While the volume covers several of the important generals and politicians—such as John Joseph Pershing and Woodrow Wilson—it also features people who played more minor roles—like Wilfred Owen, a poet and soldier, and Helen Thomas, a soldier's wife who wrote about the war. Together these entries offer students a range of perspectives by which to understand the terrible conflict known as World War I.

Additional Features

World War I: Biographies contain sidebars to highlight interesting information and more than sixty black-and-white illustrations that help to enliven the text. Each entry concludes with a list of sources—including Web sites—for additional study. A timeline, a glossary, and a subject index also are included in *World War I: Biographies*.

World War I Reference Library

World War I: Biographies is only one component of a three-part World War I Reference Library. The other two titles in this set are:

- *World War I: Almanac* (one volume) covers the war in twelve thematic chapters, each geared toward offering an understanding of a single element of the conflict, from the underlying causes of the war to the many battles fought on the various fronts to the anguished attempt to establish world peace at the war's end.

- *World War I: Primary Sources* (one volume) offers thirty-three full or excerpted documents from the World War I era. Included are Woodrow Wilson's "Fourteen Points" speech; excerpts from Ernest Hemingway's novel *Farewell to Arms;* poems from leading war poets such as Alan Seeger and Rupert Brooke; and the "Dual Alliance" secret treaty between Germany and Austria-Hungary. A sampling of propaganda posters and numerous first-person accounts from soldiers at the front are also presented.

- A cumulative index of all three titles in the World War I Reference Library is also available.

Dedication

To our children, Conrad and Louisa.

Special Thanks

We'd like to thank several people who have contributed to the creation of this book. We could ask for no better editor than Christine Slovey at U • X • L, who saw this book through most of its creation and always helped make our job easier. Dick Hetland—chair of the social studies department and teacher of twentieth-century American history at Snohomish High School in Snohomish, Washington—offered invaluable advice on how to shape the content of this book to fit the needs of students. Several writers contributed significantly to this volume: Tina Gianoulis, who can make any topic interesting; Edward Moran, who is truly gifted at digging up obscure information; and Sheldon Goldfarb.

There are many others who contributed to this book without even knowing it. They are the historians and scholars who contributed their skills to writing books and articles on one of the most tragic events in human history. Their names can be found in the bibliographies of every chapter, and our debt to them is great.

Suggestions

We welcome any comments on the *World War I: Biographies*. Please write: Editors, *World War I: Biographies*, U • X • L, Gale Group, 27500 Drake Road, Farmington Hills, Michigan, 48331-3535; call toll-free: 800-877-4253; or fax to: 248-699-8097; or send e-mail via www.galegroup.com.

World War I: Timeline

June 28, 1914 Austrian archduke **Franz Ferdinand** and his wife Sophie are assassinated by a Serbian nationalist in Sarajevo, leading to World War I.

July 31, 1914 French political leader and journalist **Jean Jaurès** is assassinated because of his antiwar position.

August 16, 1914 German quartermaster general **Erich Ludendorff** single-handedly takes the Belgian fortress at Liège and rallies German troops, earning himself the nickname "The Hero of Liège."

October 29–November 22, 1914 During the First Battle of Ypres, British general **Douglas Haig** becomes commander of the British forces.

October 12, 1915 British nurse **Edith Cavell** is executed by a German firing squad because of her involvement with the resistance movement in Belgium.

1916 British soldier **T. E. Lawrence** aids Arab leader Husayn ibn 'Alī in a revolt against the Ottoman Turks.

Franz Ferdinand and his wife Sophie. *Hulton Getty/Archive Photos, Inc.*

Wilfred Owen. *Reproduced by permission of The Granger Collection, Ltd.*

1916 British soldier and poet **Wilfred Owen** writes his most famous poem, "Dulce et Decorum Est," about the use of mustard gas against his fellow soldiers.

1916 French military and political leader **Henri-Philippe Pétain** leads victorious French troops into the Battle of Verdun.

July 4, 1916 American poet and soldier **Alan Seeger** is killed in a battle near the French village of Belloy-Santerre.

September 17, 1916 German flyer Baron **Manfred von Richthofen** shoots down his first Allied plane; he will soon become the top German air ace and earns the nickname "The Red Baron."

February 13, 1917 Dutch exotic dancer **Mata Hari** is arrested, and later executed, by the French as a German spy.

April 1917 Turkish general **Mustafa Kemal Atatürk** leads a brilliant defense of the Turkish seaport of Gallipoli against an Allied invasion.

April 6, 1917 American general **John Joseph Pershing** is chosen to command the American forces in Europe.

April 17, 1917 American journalist **George Creel** is sworn in as the chairman of the Committee on Public Information, a government agency that used the media to persuade Americans to support the war effort.

June 2, 1917 Canadian pilot **William "Billy" Avery Bishop** attacks a heavily staffed German unit at a military airport, destroying three planes and earning him the Victoria Cross.

October 5, 1917 Jewish spy **Sarah Aaronsohn** commits suicide to prevent further torture by Turkish soldiers for information regarding other Allied spies.

November 1917 Russian revolutionary and political leader **Vladimir Lenin** is named chief commissar of Russia.

November 8, 1917 Austrian violinist **Fritz Kreisler** is forbidden to perform in concert in New York at Carnegie Hall after protests by patriotic organizations, who persuade local officials to declare his appearance a threat to public safety.

An American soldier during a German gas attack. *Reproduced by permission of Hulton Getty/Archive Photos, Inc.*

1918 For his bravery and success in the war effort, American flyer **Eddie Rickenbacker** is awarded France's Croix de Guerre (Cross of War).

January 8, 1918 U.S. president **Woodrow Wilson** delivers his "Fourteen Points" address to Congress.

March 1918 After achieving success with his offensive tactics on the Italian front, French general **Ferdinand Foch** is named supreme commander of all Allied forces on the Western Front.

July 16, 1918 Russian empress **Alexandra Fyodorovna** and her family are killed by revolutionaries.

October 8, 1918 American soldier **Alvin C. York** single-handedly takes 132 German prisoners, kills 25, and disables 35 machine guns, earning himself a promotion to sergeant and numerous military medals.

November 1918 German kaiser **Wilhelm II** is forced to abdicate his thrown because of Germany's defeat during World War I.

1919 German artist **Käthe Kollwitz** creates one of her most famous drawings, *Widows and Orphans*, depicting the horrible wasting of young lives on the World War I battlefields.

1926 **Helen Thomas**, wife of slain American soldier and poet Edward Thomas, publishes the first volume of her memoirs of the war.

1926 The Reichstag Investigating Committee uses German sailor **Richard Stumpf**'s diary as evidence for the causes of two German navy mutinies during World War I.

Woodrow Wilson.
Reproduced by permission of AP/Wide World Photos.

Käthe Kollwitz *Reproduced by permission of Corbis-Bettmann.*

Words to Know

A

Allies: The nations who joined together to fight the Central Powers during World War I; they included France, Great Britain, Russia, Belgium, Italy, the United States, and several smaller countries.

Armistice: A temporary stop in fighting, or truce.

Artillery: Large-caliber weapons such as cannons and missile launchers that are capable of firing shells from a long distance.

Attrition: The gradual reduction in the strength of an army due to men being killed in battle.

B

Bolsheviks: A group of radical Russian activists who led the 1917 revolution in that country.

Bond: A certificate of debt issued by a government that promises repayment at a later date, plus interest; bonds were sold to raise money to support the war effort.

C

Campaign: A series of military operations undertaken to achieve a larger goal in war; a campaign will often consist of a number of battles.

Casualty: A soldier injured, killed, captured, or missing in the course of a battle; military strategists count casualties as a way of assessing the damage done in a battle or campaign.

Cavalry: A military body that uses horses to move about the field of battle; after World War I, which saw the end of the use of horses in warfare, cavalry was used to refer to a mobile army force that used vehicles.

Central Powers: The nations who joined together to fight the Allies during World War I; they included Germany, Austria-Hungary, the Ottoman Empire, and several smaller nations.

Chancellor: The leader of the German parliament, similar to a British prime minister.

Conscription: Forced enrollment in the armed forces; often referred to as the draft.

Convoy: A group of ships sailing together in order to provide protection from submarine attacks.

D

Diplomacy: The practice of conducting international relations, including making treaties and alliances.

Dreadnought: A large, heavily armored warship.

E

Empire: A political unit consisting of several territories governed by a single supreme authority; before World War I, several countries—including the Ottoman Empire, France, the United Kingdom, and the Austro-Hungarian Empire—were considered empires because they ruled distant colonies from their capitol.

Entente Cordiale: French for a "friendly understanding," this 1904 agreement between Britain and France promised cooperation in military affairs.

Exile: Enforced removal from one's native country.

F

Fascism: A system of government in which all authority—military, economic, and governmental—is held in the hands of a single ruler.

Flank: The side of a military formation; one army "flanked" another by attacking its side, where it was weakest.

Fleet: A group of warships under a single command.

Front: The front line of a combat force in battle; the point at which two armies meet.

G

Genocide: The organized extermination of an entire national, racial, political, or ethnic group.

I

Imperial: Having the characteristics of an empire.

Infantry: Foot soldiers; the majority of soldiers in an army, these soldiers are trained to fight and advance on foot.

Internationalism: The political belief that the world would be better off if all countries worked together to solve their problems; this was the opposite of "isolationism."

Isolationism: An American political viewpoint that held that the United States should avoid becoming involved, or "entangled," in European problems.

M

Mobilization: The act of organizing military forces in preparation for war.

Mortar: A portable cannon used to fire explosive shells at the enemy over a fairly short distance.

Mutiny: Open rebellion against authority.

N

Nationalism: Fervent commitment to one's nation.

Neutrality: An official government policy that declares that the country in question will not take sides in a war.

P

Parapet: An earthen embankment protecting soldiers from enemy fire.

Pogrom: An organized massacre or persecution of a minority group, often used to refer to the persecution of Jewish people.

R

Reformer: One who is committed to improving conditions, usually in politics or civic life.

Reparations: Cash payments for damages done during wartime.

S

Shell-shock: A form of mental distress caused by coming under fire in battle.

Shrapnel: Fragments from an explosive shell.

Siege: A blockade placed around a town or armed fortress in order to defeat those inside it.

Sniper: A skilled marksman whose job is to shoot enemy soldiers from a concealed position.

T

Theater: A broad area in which military operations are conducted.

Treaty: A formal agreement between two countries.

World War I
Biographies

Sarah Aaronsohn

1890
Zikhron Ya'akov, Palestine
October 9, 1917
Zikhron Ya'akov, Palestine

Spy

Sarah Aaronsohn's story is one of personal courage and risk to further a cause. A Jewish woman who lived in Palestine thirty years before the state of Israel was founded, Aaronsohn risked her own safety to work as an intelligence agent (spy) during World War I. She helped provide vital war information to the British, in the hopes that the British would defeat the Ottoman Turks who ruled Palestine and help the Jewish people establish a homeland there. Though she died violently as a result of her efforts, her work helped save the lives of many British soldiers. She is honored as a hero in Israel and by many Jews around the world.

Child of Refugees

Sarah Aaronsohn's Jewish parents, Ephraim and Malkah, went to Palestine in 1882 as refugees from Romania. Since the first century C.E., when Jews were forced from Palestine by the Roman Empire, Jews had moved into almost every country of the world. Wherever they went, Jews were often viewed with suspicion by non-Jews. Even in places where there had been Jewish communities for centuries, Jews were often

"You are too late. You will not be saved . . . you have tortured me in vain . . . in vain you will torture innocent people . . . you are lost . . . behold, the redeemers come . . . I have saved my people . . . my curse will follow you to the end of generations."

—Sarah Aaronsohn, speaking to her Turkish captors just before her death; quoted from http://reed.kfarolami.org.il/resources/landmark/history/nilisara.htm, edited by Avi Tsur.

Sarah Aaronsohn.

1

treated like hated foreigners. Most jobs were not open to Jews, and violent attacks, called *pogroms,* happened regularly throughout Europe. Anti-Jewish feeling was so common that it was given a special name, "anti-Semitism." Many countries, especially in eastern Europe, allowed violence against the Jews because it gave the non-Jewish population someone to blame their troubles on. If people blamed the Jews when prices were high or when crops failed, then they would not blame their own governments. Despite these difficulties, Jews carefully kept their religion and customs intact, no matter where they lived.

In the late nineteenth century, many Jews who lived in places where they were treated badly left to try to find better places to live. Many went to the United States, where equality was promised under the law. Many others immigrated to Palestine, the land of their ancestors. Ephraim and Malkah Aaronsohn and their six-year-old son Aaron were among those who immigrated to Palestine. Together with sixty-four other families from Romania, they bought 1,000 acres of land in Palestine and founded the town of Zikhron Ya'akov. Though many of them died of hardship and disease, the people who survived built a thriving community. There, in 1890, Sarah Aaronsohn was born.

A Young Woman with a Vision

Young Sarah was a strongminded and independent girl with big dreams for her country's future and her own role in it. Her childhood was not easy: Her parents had become hardened by their difficult lives, which were filled with hard work and harsh conditions, and they didn't have much time for their children. Her younger sister, Rivka, was more light-hearted than Sarah and seemed to accept the limited roles allowed to girls of her time, who were expected to become wives and mothers. Sarah wanted to be more like her brothers. Her older brother Aaron was a respected scientist, a student of agriculture who had earned a place in history by discovering an ancient wild wheat in the Galilee area of Palestine. Sarah's brother Alex led a defense patrol to guard the village against attacks from neighboring Turks and Arabs. Sarah Aaronsohn longed for her own place in history.

In the spring of 1914, Aaronsohn married a Bulgarian Jew named Chaim Abraham and moved with him to the faroff cosmopolitan city of Constantinople. Aaronsohn hated leaving her beloved homeland, and she was not happy in Constantinople. The marriage had been arranged by her father, and Sarah did not like her new husband. When World War I broke out, she longed to be home with her family, and she left Chaim and returned home to Palestine. On the long journey home, she passed through Anatolia and Syria, which at that time were part of the Ottoman Empire, as was Palestine. (The Ottoman Empire stretched across the Middle East and was controlled by the Turks, though it contained several other countries and ethnic groups.) A large population of Armenians had lived for centuries in Anatolia and Syria, as uncomfortable as most ethnic minorities under Turkish rule. When the Turks began to suspect that the Armenians were helping Russians who were invading Turkish territory, they punished the Armenians severely. Aaronsohn was horrified to witness the slaughter of thousands of Armenians at the hands of the Turks. Seeing this strongly influenced her next actions. If the Ottomans could kill more than six hundred thousand Armenians, what would prevent the same thing from happening to the Jews under Turkish rule?

Sarah and her brother Aaron, along with others like Absalom Feinberg and Yosef Lishansky, began to believe that the best hope for the Jewish people lay with the British. If the Jews helped the British invade and occupy Palestine, perhaps the British would reward the Jews by allowing them to establish a Jewish homeland in Palestine. Toward this end, they formed a secret group that would spy on the Ottoman Turks and pass useful information to the British. They named the group Nili, the first letters in the Hebrew phrase "*Netzach Israel Lo Ishaker*" ("The strength of Israel will not lie." 1 Sam. 15:29). This verse from the Bible became the password for Nili.

The Dangerous Life of a Spy

In February of 1917, Nili made its first contact with the British, in Cairo, Egypt. Over the next few months, the spies of Nili continued to collect information and pass it to the British; they usually traveled by boat from Palestine to Egypt. They knew that the risks they took were great, and after several months, Aaron begged his sister to stop working with Nili, for

Zionism: The Debate over a Homeland

Each year, on the Jewish holiday of Passover, many Jews celebrate with a ritual meal called a seder. The seder traditionally ends with participants saying "Next year in Jerusalem!" These enthusiastic words symbolize the connection of the Jewish people to the land of Palestine. However, among Jews there has always been disagreement over how literally this ritual salute should be taken.

Sarah Aaronsohn and her family were Zionists, Jews who believe that Jewish people should have a national homeland, rather than living as ethnic and religious minorities in other countries. Zionism got its start in the United States and Europe in the late nineteenth century, led by Jewish thinkers such as the Hungarian Theodor Herzl, the German Max Nordau, and the British Israel Zangwill. Constant outbreaks of antiJewish violence made life intolerable for many European Jews, and some began to think that the solution might be for Jews to create a new homeland of their own. These thinkers called themselves Zionists, because Zion was one of the names of the ancient biblical Jewish homeland.

The first Zionist World Congress took place in Basel, Switzerland, in 1897. Among the topics debated was the location of the new homeland. While some insisted that Palestine was the only logical place, others spoke in favor of areas in South America or Africa. Some questioned whether it was fair for Jewish settlers to take over a land where other people were living. Still other Jewish leaders objected to the whole idea of Zionism, saying that instead of leaving the countries they lived in and establishing a new state, Jews should fight for acceptance and full citizen rights for Jewish people in every country. More than a century after the Zionist World Congress first met, these same issues still arise as problems whenever Zionism is discussed.

her own protection. Sarah Aaronsohn refused; she felt that the work of Nili was too important to her and to the Jewish people.

In September 1917, the Turks captured a carrier pigeon with evidence of a Jewish spy ring in Palestine. When Sarah Aaronsohn learned that the Turks had discovered Nili, she helped the other members of Nili escape by remaining at home herself, to give the appearance of normality. She was at home weeks later when the Turks came and arrested her. She was tortured for three days, but she firmly refused to give her captors any information. On the fourth day, October 5, she was taken to her own house again to prepare to be transferred to the Turkish prison in Nazareth. Left alone for a few minutes and fearful that she could not withstand more torture, Sarah Aaronsohn shot herself with a gun she had kept hidden in a secret panel in her house. She died four days later.

Though most of its agents were caught and killed or imprisoned, Nili had accomplished its goal. By December 1917, the British, led by General Edmund Allenby had captured Palestine and issued the Balfour Declaration, promising to help establish a Jewish "national home" in Palestine. Unfortunately, the British also had promised the Palestinian Arabs their independence in exchange for helping the British defeat the Ottoman Turks; and all the while, the British and the French were planning to divide the region between themselves once the war was won. These contradictory promises set the stage for decades of unrest in the region, for both Jews and Palestinians lay claim to the same geographical regions known as the "Holy Land."

In Israel, the Jewish state that was eventually created in Palestine, Sarah Aaronsohn finally has her place in history. She is a national hero, whose story is taught to schoolchildren. Many people visit Sarah Aaronsohn's grave, in her hometown of Zikhron Ya'akov, on the anniversary of her death, to remember one woman's great sacrifice to help her people.

For More Information

Books

Cowen, Ida, and Irene Gunther. *A Spy for Freedom: The Story of Sarah Aaronsohn.* New York: Lodestar Books, 1984.

Engle, Anita. *The Nili Spies.* London: Frank Cass, 1997.

Web sites

Berman, Mark. "REED, edited by Avi Tsur." [Online] http://reed.kfarolami. org.il/resources/landmark/history/nilisara.htm (accessed April 2001).

Mustafa Kemal Atatürk

**1881
Salonika, in the Ottoman Empire
November 10, 1938
Istanbul, Turkey**

Military leader, political leader, statesman

The name Atatürk means "Father of the Turks," and Mustafa Kemal Atatürk earned the title by devoting his life to making positive changes in his native land. Often called the founder of modern Turkey, Atatürk was a great general who defeated invading armies and led a revolution to gain independence for Turkey. He also was a great visionary who understood the kinds of changes that would be necessary for Turkey to join the new Europe that would emerge after World War I. As president of Turkey for fifteen years, Atatürk introduced many changes and reforms in Turkish law and society. Though some Turks resisted these changes to their traditions, Atatürk is still honored in Turkey as a great hero.

Poverty and Struggle at the End of an Empire

When Atatürk was born in the old Greek city of Salonika in 1881, that city was part of the Ottoman Empire, which had been created by the Ottoman Turks in the fourteenth century. The armies of the Ottoman Empire conquered the entire Middle East and much of North Africa. By the 1500s, it had become the most powerful state in the world. When the

Ottomans tried to push westward into Europe, however, European nations banded together to stop them. After that, the empire's decline was slow but sure. Born near the end of the Ottoman Empire's sixth century, Atatürk grew up in poverty in the Turkish section of Salonika, and the miserable conditions of his life made him angry. He hated the class system that separated the rich from the poor. He hated the traditional clothes he had to wear—loose trousers and blouse with a sash—that branded him as a peasant. He hated the rigid religious schools that poor Turks attended. He hated the corrupt government officials who controlled the city. Unwilling to accept authority without questioning, he fought with his parents and his teachers as often as he fought with the Greek children in the streets of his city.

Atatürk finally refused to go to religious school and was sent to a modern, secular (nonreligious) school; there he began to wear western clothes like pants and a shirt, instead of his traditional clothes. In 1893, he entered a military school, where he was very successful. He had been given only the name Mustafa, because common people generally had no last names, but his mathematics teacher added the name Kemal, which means "perfection." Mustafa Kemal graduated in 1905 with the rank of staff captain. In military school, he had not only learned how to be a soldier, he also had learned that the government of the failing empire was dishonest and corrupt. And, from the extremely patriotic Greeks and Macedonians, he had learned about nationalism—a fierce devotion to one's nation.

Fighting for a New Turkey

Atatürk had a distinguished military career, serving all over the vast Ottoman Empire and advancing to the rank of pasha, or general. He played a major role in defending the Ottoman Empire during World War I, becoming a beloved war hero. In April 1915, he led a brilliant defense of the Turkish seaport of Gallipoli against an Allied invasion. Though defeated by the British at Megiddo in September 1918, he regrouped his forces and faced Allied troops again in October, holding a defensive line at Aleppo until an armistice (peace treaty) was signed with the British on October 30. He did not forget his early dislike of the corrupt Ottoman government, however. (The sultan was the ruler of the Ottoman Empire.)

Turks marching in Damascus, Syria, as part of the Turko-German alliance made during World War I. Atatürk led several forces such as this during the war. *Hulton Getty/Archive Photos, Inc.*

His skill on the battlefield went hand in hand with his rebellion. Early in his career he helped form a secret organization of officers called "Homeland and Freedom" to plot against the sultan. During World War I, Atatürk angered his superiors by suggesting that the army should withdraw its support from the non-Turkish parts of the empire.

Although the armistice dissolved the Ottoman army, Atatürk kept the Turkish armies together to defeat the Greeks who, encouraged by the other Allies, were invading Turkey's west coast. In 1919, Atatürk landed in the Black Sea port of Samsun to launch Turkey's War of Independence from the Ottoman Empire. On April 20, 1920, Mohammed VI, the last sultan of the Ottoman Empire, signed the Treaty of Sèvres with the Allies. This treaty gave large parts of Turkey to various Allied nations, leaving only a tiny, powerless nation that would be under Allied control. Atatürk was determined to resist the terms of the treaty and gain international recognition for a new Turkey. On April 23, 1920, the first Grand

What's in a Hat?

"We are going to adopt the modern, civilized, international mode of dress . . . including a headdress with a brim," Mustafa Kemal Atatürk told his people, according to Deane Fons Heller in *Hero of Modern Turkey: Atatürk*. When Atatürk banned the wearing of the fez, a brimless hat, in 1925, many of his fellow Turks were stunned and horrified. It may seem odd that the brim of a hat should be so important, but the fez was a meaningful symbol to the Muslim people in Turkey.

Within the Ottoman Empire, different populations had been distinguished less by nationality than by religion. Some were Jewish, others were Catholic or Orthodox, but the dominant religion of the empire was Islam. Those who practice Islam are called Muslims. Islam is a religion rich with tradition and strictly enforced customs. One of the most

sacred of these customs is that Muslim men always keep their heads covered. For centuries, men in Islamic countries have worn turbans. Because this kind of headdress covers the head while allowing the wearer to touch his forehead to the floor in prayer, the wearing of the turban became a revered tradition. In countries like the Ottoman Empire where Islam was the government as well as the religion, these traditions solidified into law. In the 1700s, the turban was replaced within the empire by the fez that served the same religious function as the turban. The fez symbolized much of what it meant to be a Muslim man, and all Muslim men wore it.

Because Atatürk wanted to separate religion and government, he felt it was necessary to end the practice of wearing the fez, to remove this symbol of the power of Islam from everyday Turkish life.

National Assembly took office with Atatürk as president. By 1923, under Atatürk's leadership, the assembly had created the Republic of Turkey, replacing the absolute monarchy of the sultan with a democratic parliamentary form of government. The Treaty of Sèvres was replaced by the more acceptable Treaty of Lausanne, which the new nationalist government signed on July 24, 1923.

Turkey's First President

During the fifteen years of his presidency, from 1923 to 1938, Atatürk worked to modernize and westernize his country. He abolished Islam as the state's religion and replaced Turkey's

Atatürk leaving Istanbul for Angora to attend the ninth anniversary celebration of the founding of the Turkish Republic. During his presidency, Atatürk worked to modernize and westernize his country.
Reproduced by permission of AP/Wide World Photos.

legal system, which was based on Islamic law, with a secular legal system. Religious leaders were stripped of much of their power. The veil worn by women and the fez, or brimless hat, worn by most Turkish men were symbols of the religious state and were therefore outlawed, to be replaced by western-style clothing. They also adopted the western calendar, which took as its reference point the birth of Jesus Christ. The Turkish language would no longer be written in Arabic script, but in the Latin alphabet used by most western nations. Atatürk himself traveled throughout the country with a blackboard to teach people how to pronounce the unfamiliar letters. He believed that a good education system was the key to a free and powerful nation, and he worked hard to improve Turkish schools.

The status of women also was improved by Atatürk's sweeping reforms. Girls were allowed to attend school, and women were given the right to vote and hold office. Atatürk also required the use of last names for everyone and founded the Institutes of Turkish History and Turkish Language. Perhaps his greatest accomplishment was that, in a land that had been a ragged remnant of a dying empire, Atatürk inspired people with pride that they were Turkish. In 1934, the parliament officially gave him the name Atatürk—Father of the Turks—in recognition of all that he had done for the Turkish people.

Not everyone welcomed the changes that Atatürk brought to Turkey, however. Many Turks were devout Muslims (the followers of Islam) who clung to the religious state and still honored the old traditions and the local religious leaders whose power Atatürk had removed. Others in Turkey resented Atatürk's intense nationalism. For example, the Kurds, a large ethnic minority living within Turkey and other nearby countries, felt that by concentrating on a Turkish identity within Turkey, Atatürk would smother the Kurdish culture. During his presidency, Atatürk defeated two Kurdish rebellions against his authority.

Though Atatürk had a great desire to make Turkey a democratic nation, he held onto a dictator's power until the end of his life. His political party, the Kemalists or People's Republican Party, was the only political party allowed. Atatürk passed and enforced his new laws not only with the strength of his powerful personality, but also with the strength of his military. However, he looked forward to a time when dictators would no longer rule in Turkey, and he had a great respect for the common people. He did not hold himself apart from the peasants and even worked side by side with other farmers on a government farm he set up on his estate near Ankara.

Atatürk always put the interests of Turkey above his personal life. He was married for only two years (1933–35) late in his life. He worked to improve conditions within Turkey up until his death, from liver disease, in 1938. Atatürk is still revered in his native land; most public buildings and many private homes proudly display his portrait.

For More Information

Books

Brock, Ray. *Ghost on Horseback: The Incredible Atatürk*. New York: Duell, Sloan and Pearce, 1954.

Heller, Deane Fons. *Hero of Modern Turkey: Atatürk*. New York: J. Messner, 1972.

Mango, Andrew. *Atatürk.* Woodstock, NY: Overlook Press, 2000.

Walker, Barbara K., Filiz Erol, and Mire Erol. *To Set Them Free: The Early Years of Mustafa Kemal Atatürk.* North Haven, Conn.: Shoe String Press, 1981.

Articles

Lawlor, Eric. "His Name Meant 'Father Turk,' and That He Was." *Smithsonian,* March 1996, 116–28.

Web sites

"Mustafa Kemal Atatürk." [Online] http://www.ataturk.org (accessed April 2001).

"Mustafa Kemal Atatürk." [Online] http://www.columbia.edu/cu/tsa/ata/ata.html (accessed April 2001).

William "Billy" Avery Bishop

**February 8, 1894
Owen Sound, Ontario, Canada
September 11, 1956
Palm Beach, Florida**

**Flying ace, head recruiting officer of
the Royal Canadian Air Force**

Canadian Billy Bishop rose to great fame as a flying ace in World War I. With seventy-two victories, Bishop was second only to the Red Baron of Germany, whose record stood at eighty downed enemy planes. Bishop maintained his enthusiasm for flying throughout his lifetime, and as director of the air force during World War II (1939–45), he recruited thousands of airmen into the Canadian air force.

Saved from School by the War

Born William Avery Bishop on February 8, 1894, in Owen Sound, Ontario, Bishop led a reckless childhood, regularly skipping school to play pool at the local YMCA. Upon graduation his academic record was not good enough to get him into a university, so he tested for the Royal Military College (RMC; the Canadian equivalent of West Point in the United States) and enrolled at the age of seventeen in 1911.

Being a cadet at the RMC did not agree with Bishop. He detested the rules and suffered severe punishment for breaking them. Once he had to clean a gun turret (a revolving structure

> "Billy Bishop was a man absolutely without fear. I think he's the only man I have ever met who was incapable of fear."
>
> —*Colonel Eddie Rickenbacker (World War I flying ace; 1890–1973), in William Arthur Bishop,* The Courage of the Early Morning: A Frank Biography of Billy Bishop.

William "Billy" Avery Bishop.

in which guns are mounted) after being late for a parade, and when the senior who inspected his work found that Bishop had missed a spider, he forced Bishop to eat it in front of the other recruits. Bishop wrote home that recruits were "the lowest form of military life, of any life, for that matter," according to his son William Arthur Bishop in *The Courage of the Early Morning: A Frank Biography of Billy Bishop*. Schoolwork did not come easily to the teenager, and he was nearly expelled for poor marks and cheating on a final exam at about the time World War I broke out. William Arthur Bishop notes that school officials described his father as "the worst cadet RMC ever had."

While at college, Bishop had given little thought to becoming a professional soldier. But in 1914 he earned a commission to the Mississauga Horse Regiment because of his military training and superior horseriding skills. A bout of pneumonia kept Bishop from going overseas until 1914, when he left for England with the Fourteenth Battalion, Canadian Mounted Rifles. Bishop soon learned the real dangers for cavalry in trench warfare and asked to be transferred to the Royal Flying Corps.

Into the Air

By 1915 Bishop had transferred to an air regiment as an observer. After his first training flight, Bishop wrote the following words, quoted in *The Courage of Early Morning* "This flying is the most wonderful invention. A man ceases to be human up there. He feels that nothing is impossible." Bishop flew on reconnaissance missions for four months before taking sick leave. He had a bad knee and a heart murmur and could have been discharged from duty. But Bishop decided he'd rather become a pilot. Within a year he earned his pilot's license and logged flying hours patrolling the southern region of England against zeppelin attacks as part of the Home Defense squadron.

In early 1917, Bishop joined the Sixtieth Squadron of the British Third Brigade, the best fighting squadron in France. He was positioned across the trenches from Manfred von Richthofen (the Red Baron, 1892–1918), the best pilot of the war and part of the "Flying Circus" of German ace pilots. The life expectancy for rookie pilots who flew against the Red Baron was about eleven days.

After four days of orientation flights, Bishop survived his first dogfight (airplane battle), downing an enemy plane. Within several weeks Bishop had become an ace (according to the French system of records, a pilot who has shot down five or more enemy planes) and had established himself as his squadron's best pilot. When Bishop was named an ace, General Hugh M. Trenchard, the commander of the Royal Flying Corps, congratulated him, saying "My boy, if everyone did as well as you've done, we'd soon win this war," as quoted by William Arthur Bishop.

Bloody April and Beyond

During April 1917, known as "Bloody April," Bishop's squadron lost thirteen of its eighteen pilots. Bishop stoically dealt with the loss of his peers. "It doesn't do to think about these things," he wrote, adding that the survivors "flew from sunup to sundown and took their fun where they could find it," according to William Arthur Bishop. During Bishop's flights that April, he won the most distinguished medals available to a soldier. Lighting an observation balloon on fire and shooting down an enemy plane near Vimy Ridge on April 8, 1917, earned Bishop his first military honor, the Military Cross. Later that month, he earned the Distinguished Service Order for singlehandedly destroying three enemy planes while being attacked by three others. Five weeks after arriving at the Western Front, Bishop had shot down seventeen enemy planes, more than any pilot in his squadron. He was promoted to captain. In his first forty days at the front, Bishop had been in almost forty air battles. By the end of May, Bishop had shot down more than twenty planes.

Flying alone in the early morning on June 2, 1917, Bishop crossed enemy lines near Cambrai and made a daring attack on a heavily staffed German unit at the Estourmel military airport. Bishop destroyed three German planes and returned unharmed to his squadron. News of his attack spread across the Western Front by that afternoon, and Trenchard sent Bishop a congratulatory message, calling his raid "the greatest single show of the war," according to William Arthur Bishop. Though some thought the pilot exaggerated his claims, French informants who had seen his attack confirmed

Canadians in World War I

When Britain entered World War I, Canada immediately guaranteed its support as well. Canada had an army of slightly more than 3,000 regular military men in 1914, but by war's end more than 619,000 Canadian volunteers had participated in World War I—a huge army for a country with a population of 8 million. Many were sent to battle with little training, but because almost half of the Canadian soldiers had been born in Britain, they had a strong sense of comradeship with their allies. Nearly 22,000 served in the British Royal Air Force.

The Canadians quickly proved their worth on the battlefield. The best Canadian initiative was the capture of Vimy Ridge along the Western Front in 1917, a turning point in the war. The battle had far fewer casualties than other attacks on the trenches, but Canadian troops gained more ground, guns, and prisoners. Brigadier General Alexander Ross led the Candian Twenty-eighth (North-West) Battalion at Vimy. Remembering the battle in a speech in 1936, he said,"It was Canada from the Atlantic to the Pacific on parade. I thought then . . . that in those few minutes I witnessed the birth of a nation," as quoted on the *Veterans Affairs Canada* Web site.

Canadians' contributions to the war effort helped Canada become recognized as an autonomous nation. The Canadian prime minister was included in official meetings such as the 1917 Imperial War Conference, and Canada was represented by its own delegates at the Peace Conference of 1919 and in the League of Nations after the war. With the passage of the Statute of Westminster in 1931, the British parliament confirmed the independent status of Canada and Canada's membership in the British Commonwealth of Nations (a group of nations of equal status that have declared allegiance to the British Crown).

the story. Bishop's actions won him the Victoria Cross, making him the first person to win all of the military's highest honors.

Bishop landed his plane in difficult circumstances many times, but his closest brush with death came during a routine patrol. German artillery hit his fuel tank, and his plane burst into flames. Able to guide the plane into Allied territory before smashing into a tree, Bishop was caught upside down with the flames of his ruined plane licking his face when a sudden rainstorm put out the flames.

By age twenty-three, Bishop was promoted to major; he had downed forty-seven enemy planes and had survived a battle with the Red Baron. Bishop was in charge of an entire squadron (Eighty-fifth Squadron, nicknamed the Flying Foxes) near Passchendaele in 1918. Within a two-week span he knocked down seventeen planes—including the German ace Paul Billik, who had thirty-one victories of his own. Bishop's stunning victories came from his fearless attacks: He would regularly charge multiple enemy planes. Once he attacked nine of the deadly Fokker D.VIIs and succeeded in downing one of them. During his last day of fighting, Bishop reportedly shot down five enemy planes, bringing his total victories to seventy-two. He returned home a national hero. Later he learned that his victories had earned him the newly created Distinguished Flying Cross.

Hero at Home

Upon his return home to Owen Sound, Ontario, Bishop was welcomed by thousands of well-wishers. For the first years after the war, Bishop traveled throughout the United States with his wife, Margaret Burden (whom he had married in 1917), giving lectures about his flying exploits and promoting his book *Winged Warfare*. When the public no longer wanted to hear his stories, Bishop spent a few years running a chartered flight business in Canada with another Canadian ace, Billy Barker. After that business failed, Bishop moved to England and began selling pipe for a French company. He amassed a sizable fortune, and he and his wife had three children. The stock market crash of 1929 left Bishop bankrupt for the second time since the war. Bishop was a good salesman, however, and soon moved his family back to Canada, where he took a position as the director of sales and promotions at the McCollFrontenac Oil Company.

World War II

In 1938, as World War II loomed, Bishop accepted the position of honorary air marshal of the Royal Canadian Air Force. As director of recruiting during the war, Bishop had a real zeal for his position. He promoted the air corps with parades, band concerts, and publicity broadcasts. He attracted more applicants than the air force could accept. He also toured

England and the United States, promoting the war. Bishop even played himself in *Captains of the Clouds,* a film released by Warner Brothers in 1942.

Bishop worked until an illness forced him into the hospital. Ignoring his doctor's warnings not to return to work, he continued recruiting airmen with the same zeal until he resigned from his post in 1944. His service earned him the Companion of the Most Honourable Order of the Bath, an award granted by the British monarchy. After his retirement from the military, Bishop wrote a second book, *Winged Peace,* in which he pondered the future of aviation. He returned to his position at McCollFrontenac Oil, but he hadn't lost his urge to serve his country; he volunteered to serve in the Korean War in 1950. The military declined his offer, and by 1952 Bishop was truly ready for retirement. He died in his sleep in the early morning of September 11, 1956, at his home in Palm Beach, Florida.

For More Information

Books

Bishop, William Arthur. *The Courage of the Early Morning: A Frank Biography of Billy Bishop.* New York: David McKay Company, 1966.

Web sites

Billy Bishop Heritage Museum. [Online] http://www.billybishop.org/index.html (accessed May 2001).

"Canada and the First World War." *Canadian War Museum.* [Online] http://www.civilization.ca/cwm/tour/trww1eng.html (accessed May 2001).

"Canada and World War I." *The History of Canada.* [Online] http://www.linksnorth.com/canadahistory/canadaandworldwar1.html (accessed May 2001).

"The First World War." *Veterans Affairs Canada.* [Online] http://www.vacacc.gc.ca/general/sub.cfm?source=history/firstwar (accessed May 2001).

Edith Cavell

December 4, 1865
Swardeston, Norfolk, England
October 12, 1915
Brussels, Belgium

Nurse, humanitarian, martyr

Accused of helping Allied prisoners escape their German captors during World War I, British-born nurse Edith Cavell was executed by a German firing squad in Brussels in 1915. Cavell had helped Belgian hospitals establish a modernized system of nursing education and patient care and had sheltered Allied soldiers in the clinic she supervised. Her death caught the notice of British propagandists (people who spread information to further or damage a cause), who portrayed this execution of a humanitarian as yet another example of German brutality. Cavell's death caused such a storm of protest that Kaiser Wilhelm (1859–1941) decreed that any future execution of a woman would require his personal approval. When Cavell's body was brought back to England after the war, bells rang and thousands of people gathered by the train tracks to honor her funeral procession as it made its way from Dover to London. Her funeral took place in Westminster Abbey on May 15, 1919, and she was buried in Norfolk, near where she had been born more than fifty years earlier.

A Bright Beginning

Edith Cavell was born in the village of Swardeston in Norfolk, England, on December 4, 1865, the eldest child of Fred-

"Edith, like Joan [of Arc], was an arch heretic: In the middle of the war she declared before the world that 'Patriotism is not enough.' She nursed enemies back to health, and assisted their prisoners to escape. . . ."

—*From George Bernard Shaw's introduction to his play* Saint Joan *(Constable, 1923), quoted in Rowland Ryder,* Edith Cavell, *p. 237.*

Edith Cavell.

erick Cavell, an Anglican priest, and his wife, Louisa Sophia Warming. Edith, whose name means "happy in war," had two sisters and a brother. The Cavells lived in a comfortable house and employed several servants. Edith, an energetic and high-spirited child, had a carefree childhood, enjoying lawn tennis, croquet, skating, swimming, and other pastimes. She also had a keen sense of observation and enjoyed studying and sketching the wildflowers that grew in abundance around Swardeston.

Edith received her early education at home, with her father as tutor, and then briefly attended a high school in Norwich. She was an exceptionally good student, and her father sent her to several boarding schools for young women, including Laurel Court in Peterborough, where she learned French and piano. After graduating, she returned home to Swardeston and taught at the Sunday school in her father's church, selling Christmas cards and her own watercolors to help raise money for the school. In 1886, Edith became a governess (nanny) for a vicar's family in Essex. Two years later, she traveled to the European continent, visiting Austria, France, and Germany.

During her European trip, Edith Cavell's humanitarian instincts first surfaced. She donated money to a hospital in Bavaria (a region in Germany) for the purchase of medical equipment and became known as the "English Angel" for her generosity. Around this time she developed an interest in becoming a nurse, though for the next few years she continued to work for several different families as a governess. In 1890 she took a job in Brussels as a governess for a prosperous family, but she returned to Swardeston five years later to take care of her ailing father. Caring for her father convinced Cavell that she should become a nurse. She was accepted into the nurse's training program at a hospital in the East End slums of London, where she remained for five years. She was devoted to her duties and helped comfort her patients with prayer and sympathetic words. During a typhoid epidemic in Maidstone in 1897, she was one of a group of nurses sent from London to take care of suffering children. Beginning in 1901, she served on the nursing staff of several hospitals that treated the poor of London. In 1907, thanks to connections she had with the family she had worked for in Brussels, Cavell received an invitation that would change her life. She was asked to become matron, or supervisor, of the Birkendael Medical Institute, Belgium's first training school for nurses.

Dedication to Duty

Edith Cavell returned to Brussels in October 1907 to begin the job of transforming a small clinic into a modern teaching hospital. She worked tirelessly to set up an excellent healthcare network that vastly improved the level of health care in Belgium, especially by providing better medical training for nurses. She helped train many nurses who went on to staff other hospitals, nursing homes, and schools around the country, including the clinic at St. Gilles Prison, where Cavell would be incarcerated after her trial in 1915. She was superintendent of the medical institute in Brussels when World War I broke out in the summer of 1914.

In the days just before World War I began, Edith Cavell was on summer vacation with her mother in England—her father had died in 1910. Hearing news of the impending war, she hurried back to Brussels, reportedly writing to one friend, "My duty is with my nurses," according to biographer Rowland Ryder. The Germans invaded Belgium in August, just days after Cavell's return to Brussels, but Cavell had been able to mobilize her staff in time to care for war casualties.

Never losing a sense of courage and cheerfulness in the face of adversity, Cavell described the horrors of the war in letters to family and friends and as a war correspondent for a British magazine read by nurses. Her commentaries evoked compassion and sympathy for the Belgian people and helped turn public opinion against the Germans even though Cavell wrote from a humanitarian and not a vengeful point of view. For example, in the magazine *Nursing Mirror,* Cavell expressed sympathy for both sides; biographer Ryder quotes her words regarding the German soldiers: "We were divided between pity for these poor fellows, far from their country and their people, suffering the weariness and fatigue of an arduous [difficult] campaign, and hate of a cruel and vindictive foe, bringing ruin and desolation on hundreds of happy homes and to a prosperous and peaceful land. . . ." About the Belgians Cavell wrote: "I can only feel the deep and tender pity of a friend within the gates, and observe with sympathy and admiration the high courage and self-control of a people enduring a long terrible agony."

Joining the Resistance Movement

After the horrific battles of Mons and Charleroi—which with their thousands of killed and injured revealed for the first time the massive destruction of modern warfare—a resistance movement developed, and numerous Belgian civilians began to secretly feed and harbor Allied soldiers and help them escape from German-occupied Belgium. Cavell became acquainted with two members of an old aristocratic family, Prince Reginald de Croÿ (1878–1961) and his wife, Princess Marie (1889–1968).

Humanitarian Organizations Assist the War Effort

When the United States entered World War I in 1917, humanitarian organizations like the American Red Cross and the Young Men's Christian Association (YMCA) rallied to the cause by expanding their services to assist soldiers and civilians injured in combat. At the request of the U.S. government, the YMCA sent chaplains overseas to minister to military personnel and to work with neutral parties in caring for prisoners of war. In 1914, when the war first broke out in Europe, the American Red Cross had only 562 chapters and about 500,000 members. By the end of the war in 1918, more than 31 million Americans—one-third of the entire population—had become members, representing every state and totaling 3,724 chapters. Even before the United States entered the war, the American Red Cross sent a mercy ship across the Atlantic to assist the wounded on both sides of the conflict. Four weeks after the United States entered the war, President Woodrow Wilson created a War Council for the Red Cross, transforming the organization into an "arm of the government," and embarked on a $100 million fundraising campaign.

During the war, the American Red Cross became known especially for setting up canteens for soldiers both at home and overseas, serving coffee and food (doughnuts were a popular item) and providing cigarettes, magazines, and snacks. Red Cross workers also offered morale-boosting words of encouragement to wounded or homesick troops.

The Red Cross also recruited 18,000 nurses, half of whom served with the armed forces in Europe and half on the home front. Letters from one of them, Helen Fairchild of Allentown, Pennsylvania, were reprinted in the *Daughters of the American Revolution Magazine* in November 1997 (also available online at http://www.ukans.edu/~kansite/ww_one/ medical/MaMh/MyAunt.htm). Fairchild served in France and Belgium during the Battle of Passchendaele during World War I. After seven months' service, she had to undergo surgery for a liver ailment, and she died of jaundice on January 18, 1918. Her letters reflect her cheerful devotion to the war effort and the importance of the contributions of humanitarian organizations. She wrote to her family that "our own U.S. boys . . . will be so far from home, and they will have no one but us American nurses to really take any genuine interest in them. . . . What the Red Cross and the YMCAs are doing for us here means so much to us. Really, it would be awful to get along without the things they send us."

For more details, see the American Red Cross Web site at www.redcross.org.

Cavell's funeral procession arriving at Victoria in London in May 1919 after her body was disinterred from its burial place in Germany. *Reproduced by permission of Archive Photos, Inc.*

The de Croÿs helped organize some of the underground resistance efforts; as a humanitarian gesture, they made sure that the Germans as well as the Allied soldiers received medical care. Cavell opened her clinic in Brussels to wounded soldiers from both sides of the conflict, but she also became part of the informal network, supported by the de Croÿs and others, that helped stranded British soldiers escape across the border to the Netherlands and eventually back to England. Cavell's clinic became a safe house where many of these men stayed while trying to get out of Belgium. Ryder quotes one of the soldiers Cavell rescued, who wrote the following words to Cavell's mother after Cavell was executed: "You will be surprised to receive this letter from me, a stranger, but had it not been for your daughter, I should undoubtedly have suffered the same fate. . . . I can only say, she has done a great deal more for her country than most of the men who are in England at present, and although I feel the deepest sympathy for you I am sure you will be proud to have such an heroic daughter."

In the summer of 1915, the Germans began threatening some members of the resistance network, but Cavell refused to leave her post at the clinic. She was taken prisoner on August 5 and locked in a cell at St. Gilles Prison. During the next few days, she signed several statements written in German admitting that she had participated in resistance activities; it is believed that the statements were not accurately translated into French for her. While awaiting trial, she drew strength from reading the *Imitation of Christ,* Thomas á Kempis's fifteenth century devotional book, and continued to write encouraging letters to the nurses at her clinic. In October, Cavell and thirty-four other prisoners, including Princess Marie de Croÿ, were put on trial. The unfair proceedings—which were conducted in German by judges who were already biased against the defendants—sent Cavell and four others to their deaths, while the other prisoners were sentenced to terms of hard labor varying from two to fifteen years; Marie de Croÿ was sentenced to ten. After writing a last, loving letter to her staff, in which she urged them to maintain their devotion to their patients and asked their forgiveness for any wrongs, Cavell was executed by an eight-man firing squad early on the morning of October 12, 1915. It was not until 1919, however, that Edith Cavell's body was disinterred (dug up) and returned to England, amidst a huge outpouring of public grief.

Edith Cavell's execution helped fuel the wartime belief that the Germans were brutal. British propagandists portrayed Cavell as the epitome (personification) of innocence and humanitarianism. Playwright George Bernard Shaw referred to Cavell in the introduction to *Saint Joan,* his play about Joan of Arc, the brave young woman who led French troops to victory over the English in the fifteenth century. Several decades after the strong feelings generated by World War I had faded, Rowland Ryder summarized the fact of Cavell's death, "It is generally assumed that Edith Cavell was sentenced to death for sheltering Allied soldiers. This is not the case. She was not sentenced to death for sheltering troops—which she had done—but for conducting soldiers [delivering injured Allied soldiers] to the enemy—which she had not done. The sentence, therefore, was not justifiable." To this day, Edith Cavell is revered, especially in Europe, as a humanitarian figure who inspired a later generation to selfless service in World War II (1939–45). In Trafalgar Square, London, a monument that honors her is inscribed with her own words: "Patriotism is not enough. I must have no hatred or bitterness for anyone."

For More Information

Books

Clark-Kennedy, A. *Edith Cavell: Pioneer and Patriot*. London: Faber, 1965.

Judson, Helen. *Edith Cavell*. New York: Macmillan, 1941.

Ryder, Rowland. *Edith Cavell*. New York: Stein and Day, 1975.

Web sites

"Edith Cavell." [Online] http://www.thehistorynet.com/BritishHeritage/articles/1997/05972_text.htm (accessed April 2001).

"Intrigue." [Online] http://www.thehistorynet.com/MilitaryHistory/articles/08964_text.htm (accessed April 2001).

George Creel

December 1, 1876
Lafayette County, Missouri
October 2, 1953
San Francisco, California

Journalist, government bureaucrat

ournalist George Creel was a pioneer in applying the tools of modern advertising and public relations to the cause of national unity during World War I. Within a week of the United States entering into the conflict, Creel was appointed by President Woodrow Wilson (1856–1924) to head the Committee on Public Information (CPI), whose mission was to create a positive image of the American war effort in newspapers, magazines, motion pictures, and other media. During the Progressive Era, just before the war, Creel had served as the editor of several newspapers that supported Wilson's reformist policies. A strong opponent of censorship, Creel urged the federal government not to impose restrictions on freedom of the press. He persuaded editors, writers, film producers, and actors to create works that presented the United States and its war effort in a favorable light. To accomplish its mission, the CPI opened offices in European cities, distributed information in several languages, and invited foreign reporters to learn first-hand of the American war effort through arranged visits to U.S. military sites and munitions factories. After the war, Creel continued to write about political issues. He also served as a

"How could the national emergency be met without national unity? The printed word, the spoken word, motion pictures, the telegraph, the wireless, cables, posters, signboards, and every possible media should be used to drive home the justice of America's cause."

—*From George Creel,* Rebel At Large: Recollections of Fifty Crowded Years, *pp. 157–58.*

George Creel.
Reproduced by permission of UPI/CorbisBettmann.

consultant on labor union issues, and he was an unsuccessful candidate for the nomination to be governor of California in 1934. However, Creel remains best known for his ground-breaking work in public information. To this day, the CPI is regarded as the forerunner of later government efforts to influence the news media, such as the Office of War Information during World War II (1939–45), as well as the United States Information Agency.

A Newspaper Man

George Creel was born in Lafayette County, Missouri, on December 1, 1876. He was the son of Henry Clay Creel, an officer in the Confederate army during the Civil War (1861–65), and Virginia Fackler Creel, a member of an old Virginia family. The Creels moved to Missouri after the Civil War, and young George went to the public schools in Kansas City. He wrote for the school newspaper but left high school before graduation to travel around the country. In 1898, he moved to New York City, where after working as a day laborer (usually an unskilled person who works for day wages), he landed a newspaper job writing for the New York *Journal*. By 1900, Creel had returned to Kansas City with his friend Arthur Grisson. The two founded a weekly newspaper, the Kansas City *Independent*, to which Creel contributed light verse and essays. Politically, Creel leaned toward leftwing (a political position advocating radical change in the government) and even socialist (shared or government ownership of production and goods) platforms, and he used his influence as a publisher to help elect the reformer Joseph Wingate Folk as governor of Missouri. Creel also published a book of poetry titled *Quatrains of Christ*.

In 1908, Creel turned over the *Independent* to two women editors and moved to Colorado, where he became an editorial writer for the Denver *Post*. After serious disagreements with the paper's owners, he returned to New York for a year to write for a number of magazines, then returned to Denver as editor of a competing newspaper, the *Rocky Mountain News*. It was during this period that he became friends with Ben B. Lindsay, a progressive judge who strongly influenced Creel's political positions. Creel soon acquired a national reputation as a muckraker, the name given to reform-minded journalists who wrote exposés of social injustice during the early twentieth century. In his editorials, Creel strongly endorsed the election of Woodrow Wilson as president in 1912. In 1914, Creel, Lindsay, and the poet Edwin Markham worked together on writing a book titled *Children of Bondage,* which criticized child labor in the United States. Two years later, when Wilson was running for reelection, Creel wrote *Wilson and the Issues,* a book that urged voters to return Wilson to the White House for a second term. Creel refused Wilson's offer of a subcabinet position (an appointed position below the cabinet level of government) out of "dislike for bureaucratic routine" but also because the move to Washington, D.C., would have caused him financial hardship.

Supporting a Free Press

When the United States finally entered World War I, Creel wrote a letter to Wilson urging him to resist the military's proposals for strict censorship of the news media. In his autobiography, *Rebel At Large,* Creel states that he believed such censorship laws to be "criminally stupid and bound to work untold harm." Arguing that "*expression,* not *suppression,* was the real need," Creel proposed instead that American newspaper editors should be the sole judges of what materials they could print. He told Wilson that it would be far more effective for the U.S. government to fight enemy spying than to impose censorship on a free press. Creel also urged the creation of a government agency that would organize a media campaign to convince all Americans to join in the war effort. On April 14, 1917, just eight days after the U.S. declaration of war, Creel was sworn in as the chairman (director) of a three-man Committee on Public Information (CPI). The other committee members were Secretary of State Robert Lansing and Secretary of War Newton Baker.

Creel's appointment was a controversial one. Lansing was disturbed by what he considered to be the "Socialistic ideas" of the new CPI director, and the *New York Times* complained in an editorial that Creel's "career had been one of turbulence and mudspattering . . . . His name stood for acrimonious contention [bitter controversy]." Despite these criticisms, Wilson allowed Creel to lead the way in creating an effective, centralized information office for the United States. Creel had, in effect, become a minister of propaganda for the United States,

TO MAKE THE WORLD A DECENT PLACE TO LIVE IN
DO YOUR PART—BUY U.S. GOVERNMENT BONDS
THIRD LIBERTY LOAN

An American propaganda poster encouraging people to buy war bonds during World War I. Creel used posters such as this to gain support for U.S. involvement in the war. *Photographed by Brown Brothers. Reproduced by permission of Archive Photos, Inc.*

but he made it clear that, in a modern democracy, the word had to be used in a different sense. In his autobiography, *Rebel At Large,* Creel states that what he advocated was "not propaganda as the Germans defined it, but propaganda in the true sense of the word, meaning the 'propagation of faith.'" In other words, Creel is making a distinction between "bad" propaganda, which he thinks is false information provided by a controlling government, and "good" propaganda, which is true information provided by a democratic government.

Informing the Public

Under Creel's direction, the CPI undertook a national public-relations campaign that enlisted the help of many prominent American writers, like Booth Tarkington, William Allen White, Ida Tarbell, and Edna Ferber, among others. These writers contributed articles about American life and democratic institutions, and the articles were translated into foreign languages and sent to news media in Europe, Latin America, and

Asia. Creel also persuaded the motion-picture industry and large corporations to create newsreel films that showed America in a positive light. In so doing, Creel used some of the modern techniques of persuasion that were being developed by the advertising industry. To encourage public support for the military draft, for example, Creel asked movie theaters across the country to show patriotic slides and interrupt their shows for brief speeches by recruiters who were called "Four Minute Men" (this was a clever phrase that not only described the brief recruiting pitches but also called to mind the patriots in the American War of Independence). The campaign was highly successful.

The CPI also invited Allied journalists to visit military bases, shipyards, and munitions factories in the United States so that they would write positive articles about the American war effort and boost morale in their own countries. "Before the flood of our publicity, German lies were swept away," Creel later wrote. The CPI also reached out to many ethnic groups in the United States to make sure that recent immigrants supported the American war effort and not that of their former homelands in Europe. The CPI even opened offices in Europe and set up a worldwide cable and wireless network to distribute articles, speeches, and other information favorable to the United States and the Allied cause. "For the first time in history," Creel later wrote, "the speeches of a national executive were given universal circulation" and within twenty-four hours were translated into every modern language. "Our war progress, our tremendous resources, the acts of Congress, proofs of our unity and determination, etc., all went forth for the information of the world."

Unlike some of his counterparts in other Allied nations, Creel refused to distribute stories of German atrocities (extremely brutal acts), even though some people criticized his decision on this point. Instead, he tried to combat anti-German feelings in the United States, maintaining that the CPI "has never preached any doctrine of hate, for it is not our duty to deal in emotional appeals but to give the people the facts from which conclusions may be drawn." When Wilson formulated his Fourteen Points plan providing a framework for peace in the postwar world, Creel transmitted it to Russia and Germany and "plastered [the Fourteen Points] on billboards in every Allied and neutral country."

Anti-German Hysteria in the United States

When George Creel began his public information campaign on behalf of the U.S. war effort during World War I, the United States had never before sent its soldiers to fight on European soil. A wave of hysteria directed against Germany and Austria-Hungary swept the nation, and many Americans directed their hatred against people from those countries, calling the Germans "Krauts" and the Austrians "Huns." Some local governments passed "English-only" laws; many high schools stopped teaching the German language; and many orchestras stopped playing music by Beethoven, Brahms, and other German composers. The Vienna-born violinist Fritz Kreisler was on a concert tour in the United States when the war broke out, and he was forbidden to play in many cities. Some people even suggested using the term "Liberty cabbage" instead of the German word "sauerkraut" and substituting "Salisbury steak" for the word "hamburger."

In the decades immediately before the war, many people from Europe, including Germany and Austria-Hungary, had immigrated to the United States. Some Americans feared that these newer immigrants might be more loyal to their old homelands than to the United States. Under George Creel's direction, the Committee of Public Information made special efforts to reach out to these immigrant communities and publicized the contributions that immigrants were making to the war effort, such as volunteering for the armed services or buying Liberty Bonds. Creel strongly criticized so-called patriotic organizations for harassing immigrants and questioning their loyalty.

The CPI angered many people, including CPI member Robert Lansing, who thought Creel's use of actors, filmmakers, and journalists was undermining the traditional role of U.S. diplomats. Creel countered this criticism by arguing that "We wanted plain Americans who thought regularly and enthusiastically in terms of America, and who would worry over doing the job, not whether they had on the right coat." Still, in 1918 Congress voted to cut the CPI's budget in half, but not before the agency had created a modern and influential public-information program for the United States, one that would serve as a model for democracies worldwide.

A Lifelong Writer

After World War I, Creel resumed his writing career. He contributed articles to major American magazines and newspapers and wrote books about Ireland and Mexico, as well as biographies of Thomas Paine and Sam Houston. In 1934, he was defeated in an attempt to win the nomination for governor in California. Creel also served as an official with the Works Progress Administration (WPA), an agency that helped find work for the unemployed during the Great Depression of the 1930s. During World War II, he criticized the Office of War Information for its wasteful spending, arguing that the CPI had accomplished the same tasks during World War I for much less money. His book *War Criminals and Punishment,* condemning German dictator Adolf Hitler and his Nazi Party, was published in 1944. Creel died on October 2, 1953.

For More Information

Books

Creel, George. *How We Advertised America: The First Telling of the Amazing Story of the Committee on Public Information That Carried the Gospel of Americanism to Every Corner of the Globe.* New York and London: Harper and Brothers, 1920.

Creel, George. *Rebel At Large: Recollections of Fifty Crowded Years.* New York: G. P. Putnam's Sons, 1947.

Knock, Thomas J. *To End All Wars: Woodrow Wilson and the Quest for a New World Order.* New York: Oxford University Press, 1992.

Mock, James R., and Cedrik Larson. *Words That Won the War: The Story of the Committee on Public Information, 1917–1919.* New York: Russell and Russell, 1968.

Web sites

"George Creel on the Selling of the War." [Online] http://web.mala.bc.ca/davies/H324War/Creel.SellingWar.1920.htm (accessed May 2001).

"Perspectives [on Military History]." [Online] http://www.thehistorynet.com/MilitaryHistory/articles/12955_text.htm (accessed May 2001).

Alexandra Fyodorovna

June 6, 1872
Darmstadt, Hesse, Germany
July 16, 1918
Yekaterinburg, Russia

Empress of Russia

"She was shy. She was warm. She was hysterical. She was a saint. She was a wife, a mother, and an empress. Above all, she was misunderstood. She was a woman who would change the course of modern history."

—From Greg King,
The Last Empress.

Alexandra Fyodorovna.
Reproduced by permission of Archive Photos, Inc.

Alexandra Fyodorovna was czarina, or empress, of Russia during a very turbulent time in history. Her husband, Czar Nicholas II, was a weak ruler with little interest in matters of state, and he was easily influenced by his strong-willed wife. Because Alexandra influenced the czar, who had absolute power over the lives of millions, the mistakes she made were magnified to huge proportions. Many people say that Alexandra was shallow and conceited. They blame her for prolonging the suffering of the Russian people and causing the fall of the czars of Russia. Others say that she was the product of a weak and corrupt system of royal families, but that she was basically a good woman who tried desperately to care for her family.

The Tragic Young Princess

Alexandra Fyodorovna had royalty on both sides of her family. She was born Alix Victoria Helene Luise Beatrix, the daughter of Princess Alice of Great Britain and Ireland and Grand Duke Louis of HesseDarmstadt, Germany. Little Alix was the sixth of seven children, and her early childhood was a happy one. Her mother was one of the daughters of Queen Victoria. Although Princess Alice had left England to live in her husband's country, she never abandoned her British roots. She passed her love of her homeland on to her children, who relished visiting their grandmother the queen in her castles in London and Scotland.

Alix's carefree childhood came to a sudden end when she was six years old. Her younger sister, May, died in a diphtheria (a serious contagious disease caused by bacteria) epidemic. Then, after nursing the rest of the family through the disease, Alix's mother died of diphtheria as well. Little Alix had been very attached to her mother and younger sister, and she was deeply affected by both deaths. Though she was still warmly devoted to her family, she withdrew into herself somewhat and from then on tended toward seriousness and deep thoughts. She was shy and mistrustful of those outside her own family and stayed that way the rest of her life.

Alix was educated at home by governesses and tutors. Her mother had been a generous woman who had worked for charitable causes, and Alix continued her mother's work helping the poor. She also became deeply religious and she joined the Lutheran faith when she was sixteen. Shortly afterwards, she was formally presented to society and stepped into the role of princess of Hesse (a southwestern region of Germany). In 1892, misfortune visited Alix's family once again. Her father died of a heart attack at the age of fifty-five, leaving the young princess an orphan.

A Royal Marriage

Alix was twenty the year her father died, and the search was soon on among her royal relatives to find her a suitable husband. Her grandmother, Queen Victoria had hoped that Alix would marry Alix's wild young English cousin Prince Albert or Prince Maximilian of Baden, a member of the German royal family. However, Alix refused to cooperate. She had no interest in those princes or in anyone else her family suggested. Her eyes were turned toward another second cousin, much farther away, in Russia.

The royal families of Europe had many connections, by blood and by marriage. Among Alix's godparents were the czar and czarina of Russia, and Alix's sister Elizabeth had married Serge, the czar's brother. At the wedding, Alix met the young czarevich, or prince, Nicholas Aleksandrovich of the noble Romanov family. In 1889, she saw Nicholas again when she went to Russia to attend a winter ball and stayed through the summer. As Alix's affection for Nicholas grew, so did her grandmother's distress. Both Queen Victoria and Nicholas's father, Alexander III, the Russian czar, were determined that Alix and Nicholas should not marry. Alix's family felt that the Russian state was too far away and too unstable. Alexander II, Nicholas's grandfather, had been assassinated by rebels, and Queen Victoria worried that Alix might be in danger if Alix became a member of Russian royalty. The czar's family, on the other hand, felt that Alix's position as princess of Hesse was not high enough for her to become the empress of Russia. For both families, the question of religion also made the situation seem hopeless: Alix was a devout Lutheran; but the state religion in Russia was Russian Orthodoxy, and the wife of a future czar had to be Orthodox.

One by one, these objections were overcome. Alexander, the old czar, grew very ill. As it became obvious that he was dying, Alexander became anxious to see his son married and settled. Nicholas was a spoiled, rich young man, with little preparation to take leadership of his country; his father felt that Nicholas needed at least a wife and family to support him, even if that wife was not quite as royal as the czar might have wished. On April 20, 1894, Nicholas proposed to Alix, who accepted and agreed to convert to the Orthodox religion (Alexandra Fyodorovna was the name she took when she converted). Once the engagement was settled, Queen Victoria finally gave the couple her blessing.

Nicholas and Alexandra were married on November 26, 1895, only a week after the funeral of Nicholas's father, Czar Alexander III. But even that solemn circumstance could not conceal the fact that they were very much in love.

The Empress

At her new Russian home in the capital city of St. Petersburg, Alexandra would always be more successful as a wife and mother than as an empress. She loved and supported her husband as he took on the new role of czar, but she did not get along with the other members of the royal family. She also

Although she was a supportive wife and mother, Empress Alexandera Fyodorovna was not a favorite with the people of Russia. *Reproduced by permission of Hulton Getty/Archive Photos.*

did not make a good impression on Russian noble society or on the peasants she ruled. Though warm by nature, she was cool and distant with those outside her family. She immediately began to isolate herself and her husband from the people, refusing to appear in public and discouraging Nicholas from doing so. Because her shyness was interpreted as pride and snobbishness, she quickly grew unpopular.

As Queen Victoria had feared, Russia was experiencing revolutionary change during this period. While the Russian court lived in extravagant luxury, in lavish castles filled with rich furs, gold, and jewels, the majority of Russian peasants and workers lived in poverty. To make matters worse, the working people of Russia suffered greatly when the Japanese defeated the Russian army in the Russo-Japanese War in 1905. The war losses triggered a series of bloody riots that were the beginnings of a revolution against the absolute rule of the czars. The revolution of 1905 ended when the czar signed an imperial manifesto, or statement, promising an elected parliament and other freedoms to the Russian people. These changes did not come quickly enough, however, and the seeds of a greater revolution took root throughout Russia.

Alexandra had been a softhearted girl, sympathetic to the poor, but the longer she lived in the imperial court of Russia, the more she changed. She became convinced that a strong hand was needed to rule, and she encouraged her husband to deal harshly with those who rebelled against his authority. Nicholas remained a weak and reluctant ruler, and he was only too happy to look to his wife for advice. Alexandra's harsh attitudes made her even more unpopular with the Russian people.

Alexandra and Nicholas had five children: four girls—Olga, Tatiana, Marie, and Anastasia—and one boy, Alexis. Alexis was born last, in August 1904, and he was welcomed with delight by his parents and sisters. However, even this happy event was shadowed with difficulties. Alexis had hemophilia, a hereditary disease in which the blood does not clot. Sometimes called "bleeders," hemophiliacs suffer extreme pain and loss of blood at the slightest bruise or cut. Alexandra was heartsick over her son's illness, and she hovered over him protectively. She took him to doctors and to priests, looking for help.

In 1905 the desperate empress thought she had found the help she sought: A noblewoman introduced her to a Siberian peasant holy man who supposedly had healing powers. The man's name was Grigory Rasputin (1872–1916). Rasputin was a dramatic figure. A large man with shaggy black hair and beard, he had a powerfully hypnotic presence. Many people have thought that Rasputin was a sort of con man, but his presence and his prayers seemed to have had a healing effect

on the young Alexis. The grateful empress made Rasputin an important part of her household and looked to him for advice on all things, even governmental decisions. This governmental advice she passed on enthusiastically to her husband, the czar. As Alexandra became more and more dependent on the man people called "the mad monk," she isolated herself even further from the Russian people.

War and Revolution

In 1914, Germany declared war on Russia. World War I was a very unpopular war in Russia, and it brought Alexandra's popularity to its lowest level. Because she had come from Germany, the Russian people suspected her of treason and scornfully called her "the German woman." Poorly led and in political confusion, Russia was not prepared for war, and things went badly for the Russian armies. Thousands were killed, and commoners and nobles alike grew angrier at the interference of Alexandra and Rasputin in government affairs.

The Romance of Anastasia

Not long after the assassination of the royal family in Yekaterinburg, rumors spread in Russia and throughout Europe that one or two of Nicholas and Alexandra's children had survived. One reason for these rumors was that those who killed the royal family had hidden their bodies. When the bodies were finally found in 1979, the bodies of Anastasia and Alexis were not among them, and some people began to hope that the czar's two youngest children might have lived. One rumor told of a kindhearted soldier who had hidden the young grand duchess and helped her escape the fate of her family. This romantic story has been the basis for plays, novels, and movies.

Over the years, several women have claimed to be the lost grand duchess Anastasia. One such woman, Anna Anderson, even convinced several members of the Romanov family that she was one of them. However, after she died in 1984, scientists developed DNA testing as a way of proving blood relationships. In 1993, when Anna Anderson's DNA was compared to that of England's Prince Philip, a distant Romanov cousin, it was finally proven that she could not have been Anastasia.

Most historians feel certain that Anastasia died along with the rest of her family, but the story of her escape still has appeal for many.

By 1917, things had only gotten worse. Supply routes had been cut off by the fighting, and peasants and workers had little money and almost no food. On International Women's Day, March 8, 1917, striking workers joined with starving peasants to protest the war and demand food. The protests grew as peasants and workers were joined by soldiers who had rebelled against their officers. Soon the rioters had taken over St. Petersburg and stormed the czar's palace. By March 15, Nicholas abdicated, giving up the role of czar for himself and any hope of his son's future rule. Alexandra was no longer empress.

The revolutionaries arrested the royal family. Nicholas, Alexandra, and their children were first held in the castle of Tsarskoye Selo, south of St. Petersburg, then moved to the Siberian town of Tobolsk. Finally they were moved to the town of Yekaterinburg, where they were held in a merchant's house that had been taken over and renamed the "House of Special

Purpose." Here they tried to maintain a family life, reading and playing games. Alexandra kept a daily journal and, always the loving mother, worried over Alexis.

Russia was in a civil war, as the supporters of the aristocracy (the White Army) tried to defeat the peasants and workers (the Red Army). The White Army approached Yekaterinburg, and it appeared that they might capture the town. Before fleeing Yekaterinburg, the Reds who were holding the royal family prisoner took the whole family into the basement of the House of Special Purpose and shot them, bayoneting the children to make sure they were dead. Though there are conflicting reports of the actual executions, it is certain that Alexandra was killed on that terrible night in 1918.

For More Information

Books

King, Greg. *The Last Empress.* New York: Birch Lane Press, 1994.

Kurth, Peter. *Tsar: The Lost World of Nicholas and Alexandra.* Boston: Little, Brown, 1995.

Massie, Robert K. *Nicholas and Alexandra.* New York: Atheneum, 1967.

Meyer, Carolyn. *Anastasia, the Last Grand Duchess.* New York: Scholastic, 2000.

Mouchanow, Marfa. *My Empress: Twenty-Three Years of Intimate Life with the Empress of All the Russias.* New York and London: John Lane, 1918.

Articles

Smith, Kyle. "Tragic Child: Anastasia's Story Is Out of Toon with the New Film." *People,* 12 January 1998, 67–70.

Films

Nicholas and Alexandra. Produced by Simon Welfare and Michael Beckham and directed by Michael Beckham. New York: Granite Film, Granada Television Production, in association with A&E Network, 1994.

Web sites

Buxhoeveden, Baroness Sophie. "Aleksandra Feodorovna." *Russian History Websites.* [Online] http://www.alexanderpalace.org/alexandra (accessed February 2001).

Franz Ferdinand

December 18, 1863
Graz, Austria
June 28, 1914
Sarajevo, Bosnia

Political leader

It is a sad fact that the best-remembered detail of the life of Franz Ferdinand is his death. Archduke Franz Ferdinand was the nephew of Austrian emperor Franz Josef (1830–1916) and the last heir to the throne of the Austro-Hungarian Empire. Bosnia and Herzegovina was a province of the Austro-Hungarian Empire. While visiting the provincial capital of Sarajevo on official business, the archduke and his wife, Sophie, were killed by a Serbian named Gavrilo Princip (1894–1918). Princip belonged to a political group that was angered by Austro-Hungarian domination of Bosnia and Herzegovina. He felt that assassinating a high official of the empire would help Serbia's cause. Serbia was a country that wanted to unite the region—including Bosnia and Herzegovina—and gain independence from Austria-Hungary. However, the deaths of the archduke and his wife only caused the Austrian emperor to respond with angry demands and finally a declaration of war on Serbia. This declaration set off a complex chain of events that led the world into World War I. Franz and Sophie Ferdinand have been called the first casualties of that war.

An Heir by Chance

Though Franz Ferdinand was born into the royal family of the Habsburgs on December 18, 1863, in Graz, Austria, he did not grow up as the heir to the throne. During the early part of his life, he was only the third in line to rule the empire, behind the emperor's son, Archduke Rudolf, and Ferdinand's own father, Archduke Carl Ludvig. A shy child, Ferdinand was educated at home by private tutors. He was intelligent and a very strict Catholic. However, many people—including some within his own family—considered him spoiled, cold, and conceited, and he had few friends.

In 1883, Franz Ferdinand joined the army and served in various places around the empire. He advanced through the ranks from lieutenant to general in just a little more than ten years. Tragedy struck the royal family in 1889, when Archduke Rudolf, the heir to the throne, killed himself. Though the emperor had a daughter, Archduchess Elizabeth, she could not rule under the law of the empire because she was a woman. Franz Ferdinand's father was the next in line for the throne, but he died in 1896, leaving his son Franz to be the emperor's heir.

A Royal Romance

Ferdinand had just been promoted to major in the imperial army when he met a Czech woman, Sophie Chotek von Chotkowa und Wognin, at a dance in Prague in 1888. The two fell in love, and Ferdinand approached his family with his plans to marry Sophie. The royal family were not pleased with Ferdinand's choice, because, though Sophie was the Duchess of Hohenberg in her own country, the proud Habsburgs considered her little better than a commoner, certainly not good enough to marry the heir to the throne of the empire.

Ferdinand fought for his bride, and he was eventually allowed to marry Sophie. But he had to agree to several things that would limit her power within the empire. First, Sophie would never be given the title of empress, and her children would not be heirs to the throne. She would not even be allowed to sit next to her husband in his carriage or in the royal box at the opera. In spite of these humiliating requirements, Sophie and Ferdinand were happily married in 1900

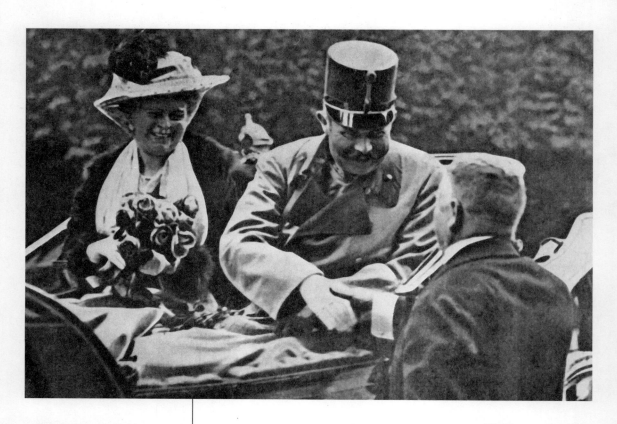

Franz Ferdinand and his wife Sophie in a carriage during their visit to Sarajevo. Both of them were killed by an assassin just minutes after this photo was taken. *Reproduced by permission of Hulton Getty/Archive Photos, Inc.*

and had three children. Ferdinand loved his wife very much, and with the family they created, he seemed to find a peace and happiness that he could never find elsewhere.

The Explosive Politics of the Empire

Outside his domestic life, however, Ferdinand remained unpopular, with a reputation for being arrogant and hot-tempered. Besides disliking his personality, many in the empire disagreed with his political views. One particularly controversial idea he had was called "Trialism." Under this plan, the Austro-Hungarian Empire, already considered a dual empire because it was ruled by an Austrian emperor and a Hungarian king, would have a third branch. This third branch of power would be given to the Slavic peoples of southeastern Europe who had been living under the rule of the empire. Some Slavs supported the notion of Trialism, but others, who hated Austro-Hungarian rule, were angered by it.

It may seem surprising that Ferdinand's wish to give the Slavic people a greater voice made him an enemy to Slavs who wanted independence from the empire. But to Serbian nationalists, who wanted their country to be completely independent of Austro-Hungarian rule, the archduke's idea was dangerous because limited power might make Slavic people more comfortable within the empire, and they might no longer wish to fight for independence. Serbian nationalists, represented by militant groups like the Black Hand, wanted to unite the Slavic people in an independent pan-Slavic state. The fact that Ferdinand was a major supporter of Trialism, coupled with the fact that he would one day inherit the throne of the empire, made him a target for the rage of the Serbian nationalist movement.

Murder in Sarajevo

In 1913, Ferdinand was appointed inspector general of the Austrian army. In 1914, he was invited to Sarajevo by the colonial governor, General Oscar Potiorek (1853–1933), to observe military exercises. Because the Serbs had been increasingly hostile to the empire, the Serbian prime minister, Nicola Pašiæ, sent a warning to Vienna that someone might try to assassinate the archduke if he came to Sarajevo. In spite of this, Franz and Sophie Ferdinand went to Sarajevo on June 28, 1914. The date was significant for two reasons. First, it was St. Vitus Day, a religious holiday when the Serbs celebrated their resistance to the Ottoman Turks. Second, it was Ferdinand and Sophie's wedding anniversary. Many people think that the nationalistic feelings of the Serbs were especially roused on their patriotic holiday. And many also think that a major factor in Ferdinand's insistence on going to Sarajevo was his affection for Sophie. Outside of Vienna, she could ride in the car beside him and receive all the attention and ceremony that she was denied at home.

As the archduke and his wife drove down a well-publicized parade route in an open car; seven assassins waited in the crowd, each armed with a pistol and cyanide, a poison they could use to commit suicide if they were caught. One of the assassins threw a bomb at the car, but it missed the target and blew up under the car behind it, injuring several people. Amazingly, Ferdinand and Sophie arrived safely at city hall and listened to a flattering speech by the mayor before deciding to go

The Changing Judgments of History

Who is the hero of this story, and who is the villain? History does not provide a clear answer.

After the assassinations of Archduke Franz Ferdinand and his wife, the Austrian government erected a monument on the spot where they were killed. A bronze plaque bearing their pictures remained there as a memorial until 1953. In that year, Josip Broz Tito (1892–1980), the leader of the young nation of Yugoslavia made up of various Slavic countries, removed the monument and opened a museum to honor Gavrilo Princip and the Young Bosnia movement, a Slavic nationalist movement. Tito led a country that had recently liberated itself from German Nazi occupation during World War II, and he wanted to elevate early Slavic nationalists like Princip to the status of heroes. The place where Princip stood to fire the fatal shots was marked with concrete footprints.

But Princip's stature as a hero did not last. A new wave of political unrest swept through Yugoslavia in the early 1990s, resulting in the breakup and restructuring of that country; Bosnia and Herzegovina declared its independence, and in this new political climate Princip was no longer considered a hero of Slavic nationalism, but rather a terrorist. Princip's footprints were removed, and so was the museum honoring him and the Young Bosnians who attacked the archduke. Some officials want to restore the original monument to the archduke, bringing the cycle back to its beginning almost a hundred years later and proving that history, even when set in concrete, can continue to change.

back by a fast and direct route to avoid more trouble. Unfortunately, those in charge did not tell the archduke's driver about the route change. He made a wrong turn and was forced to back up into an alley to turn around. Most of the assassins, including nineteen-year-old Gavrilo Princip, had given up and left when the bomb missed its mark. However, when the car slowed to back into the narrow alley, Princip found himself only a few feet from the archduke, the uniformed symbol of the hated Austro-Hungarian rulers. Princip raised his gun and fired two shots, killing Ferdinand and Sophie. He later said that he had intended his second bullet for Potiorek and was sorry he had killed Sophie.

For More Information

Books

Brook-Shepherd, Gordon. *Archduke of Sarajevo: The Romance and Tragedy of Franz Ferdinand of Austria.* Boston: Little, Brown, 1984.

Cassels, Lavender. *The Archduke and the Assassin.* New York: Stein and Day, 1984.

Pauli, Hertha Ernestine. *The Secret of Sarajevo: The Story of Franz Ferdinand and Sophie.* New York: AppletonCentury, 1965.

Articles

DeVoss, David. "Searching for Gavrilo Princip." *Smithsonian,* August 2000, 42–46.

Films

From Mayerling to Sarajevo. Produced by Eugene Tuchener and directed by Max Ophuls, 1997. Videocassette.

Web sites

"Archduke Franz Ferdinand." *World War I: Trenches on the Web.* [Online] http://www.worldwar1.com/biohff.htm (accessed April 2001).

"The Assassination of Archduke Franz Ferdinand." [Online] http://www.k12.nf.ca/randomisland/ww1/franz.htm (accessed April 2001).

"Franz Ferdinand." [Online] http://www.spartacus.schoolnet.co.uk/FWWarchduke.htm (accessed April 2001).

Ferdinand Foch

October 4, 1851
Tarbes, France
March 20, 1929
Paris, France

Military leader

Ferdinand Foch. *Photograph courtesy of The Library of Congress.*

Marshal Ferdinand Foch had a great influence on the French military during his lifetime. Head of the national military academy for three years, he led several French regiments in many of the critical battles of World War I. Near the end of the war he was made head of all the Allied armies, and his bold strategies and strong will helped ensure the victory over Germany in 1918. Though many have disagreed with his philosophy and his tactics, Foch is still viewed as the single person most responsible for the Allied victory in World War I.

Dreams of War

Ferdinand Foch was born in the town of Tarbes, at the foot of the Pyrenees mountains in southwestern France, on October 4, 1851. His family was solidly middle class and had lived in the region for generations before Ferdinand and his sister and two brothers were born. Ferdinand's father, Bertrand Foch, was a lawyer and civil servant (a person employed by the government). Strict and demanding, he was not a harsh man, but one who loved his children and expected hard work and good behavior from them. Ferdinand's mother, Sophie, was kindhearted, though like her husband, she believed in teaching discipline and religious devotion.

At a very early age, Ferdinand Foch began to long for the life of a soldier. His mother's father had been a soldier in the army of Emperor Napoléon I (1769–1821), the flamboyant French military leader. Foch reveled in the war stories told by his great-aunt Jenny Nogues, who had been married to a soldier in Napoléon's army. Foch listened for hours while his great-aunt told stories of the battles and adventures of the dashing Napoléon, one of France's great heroes. While he learned about the great battles, Foch also learned about Napoléon's strong personality and great force of will, both of which made Napoléon a powerful leader. Napoléon embodied a characteristic that Foch would come to value highly. In French it is called *élan,* which means spirit and energy plus a little showmanship and flash. Foch would come to believe that *élan* was one of the most important qualities for achieving military victory.

Because his parents wanted him to have a solid religious foundation, Foch was educated by Roman Catholic monks, first at a seminary near Tarbes, then at St. Michel, a Jesuit college in the town of Saint-Étienne, where his father had gone to work. Foch was always an excellent student, winning prizes and impressing his teachers with his accomplishments. In 1869, he attended the Jesuit school of St. Clement in the town of Metz and began to come closer to his dream of being a soldier.

Metz is in northern France in a region called Alsace-Lorraine; control of this region had long been disputed by France and Germany. In the summer of 1870, when Foch was with his family between school terms, war broke out between the two countries. The school at St. Clement's was temporarily closed, and nineteen-year-old Foch enlisted in the army. The Franco-Prussian War ended in January 1871, but Foch, though ready and eager to defend his country, had never been sent into battle.

He began to understand some of the pain of war, however, when he returned to school at St. Clement's. As a result of the war, Metz now belonged to Germany, and Foch was angered and shamed to see German soldiers striding boldly through the streets of the town he considered to be French. The time he spent in Metz under German occupation left him

Hôtel des Invalides, Resting Place of Heroes

When Marshal Ferdinand Foch died, there was not only a solemn funeral mass in Paris, but there were memorials honoring him as far away as London and Washington. Even his old enemies in Germany sent messages honoring him. As perhaps the most fitting tribute, his body was buried in a tomb under the dome of *Hôtel des Invalides* in Paris, where his boyhood hero, Napoléon I, was also buried.

The *Hôtel des Invalides* was originally built in 1671 as a hospital for disabled veterans. Its spectacular dome was designed by Jules Hardouin Mansart. The soaring expanse supported on classical columns is meant to represent the power of the nation supported by the institutions of its government.

Eventually the hospital became a museum of French military history, and *Hôtel des Invalides* has remained one of the most revered of French shrines. Under the dome, several of France's most beloved military leaders have been buried. In 1675, Marshal Henri de La Tour Turenne was buried there, and in 1707, Sébastien Vauban, a famous military engineer, joined him. But perhaps the most honored tomb is that of Emperor Napoléon I. Finally defeated by the British in 1815, Napoléon had been exiled to the British colony island Saint Helena, where he died in 1821. In 1840, Napoléon's remains were brought home to Paris and buried with honor under the dome of *Hôtel des Invalides.*

with a lifelong dislike of Germans, and it renewed his desire to be the kind of military hero who could liberate France.

War College

In 1871, after graduating from St. Clement's, Foch attended the École Polytechnique (Polytechnic School), a military school in Nancy, another formerly French city that had been occupied by Germany since the Franco-Prussian War. Graduating in 1874 with the rank of second lieutenant of artillery, Foch was finally where he had wanted to be all of his life—in the army. He served at various garrisons in France for the next ten years, then decided to continue his education by entering the École Supérieure de la Guerre (War College) in 1885.

In 1895, after serving in a variety of staff positions, including two appointments with the General Staff, Foch returned to the War College to teach strategy. He taught for many years, developing a philosophy of war that was exciting to students and fellow teachers alike. Foch favored an offensive approach to fighting. He still placed a lot of importance on *élan* and the will to win, but he also taught that flexibility was an important quality of a good military leader and that a commander needs to inspire confidence and a positive attitude in his men. Foch's lectures were so respected that they were collected and published as *The Principles of War* in 1903 and *The Conduct of War* in 1904. By 1908, Foch had risen to the rank of general and was appointed head of the War College from 1908 to 1911.

A Military Hero

In 1913, Foch, already at retirement age, took command of the French Twentieth Army at Nancy. When World War I broke out, he did such a good job defending against a German

Foch (left) riding in a car with American general John Pershing during a parade honoring Foch's arrival in the United States.

attack there that he was given command of another force, the Ninth Army, which fought in the first battle of the Marne in early September 1914. In that battle and in later ones, such as the first battle of Ypres (October 19 to November 22, 1914) and the battle of the Somme (July 1 to November 13, 1916), Foch's offensive tactics caused the loss of many French lives. His strategy of aggressive attacks did not work well against the Germans, who were heavily armed with the most modern weapons. Other generals began to blame Foch because the war was going badly for France. As a result, Foch's command was taken from him, and he was removed from active service for several months while other generals, such as RobertGeorges Nivelle (1856–1924) and Philippe Pétain (1856–1951), replaced him on the front.

In 1917, Foch was called back to active duty and made chief of the French general staff. He led his troops so successfully on the Italian Front that in March 1918 he was appointed supreme commander of the British, American, and French armies. Though he had some conflict with the American general John J. Pershing (1860–1948), Foch used skill and training to coordinate the Allied efforts, and he masterminded an Allied counterattack against Germany that brought about the end of the war. On November 11, 1918, Foch, who had been promoted to marshal of France on August 6, accepted the German surrender.

Foch was present when the Treaty of Versailles was negotiated to end the war, and he was appointed head of the military committee charged with enforcing the terms of the treaty. He felt that the treaty should have given Germany even harsher punishment to prevent the rise of German military power in the future. Frustrated that his advice was not taken, Foch predicted another European war with Germany at its center within twenty years.

Perhaps fortunately, Foch did not live to see the truth of his prediction. At the age of seventy-seven, he died of a heart attack in Paris on March 20, 1929. He had continued to work for France almost until the day of his death.

For More Information

Books

Aston, Sir George. *The Biography of the Late Marshal Foch.* New York: Macmillan, 1929.

Foch, Ferdinand. *The Principles of War.* Trans. J. De Morinni. Reprint, New York: A M S Press, 1970.

Hart, B. H. *Foch, the Man of Orléans.* London: Penguin, 1937.

Articles

Bradley, Dermot. "Ferdinand Foch." In *The Harper Encyclopedia of Military Biography.* New York: Harper, 1992.

Web sites

Fenton, Damien. "Unjustly Accused: Marshal Ferdinand Foch and the French 'Cult of the Offensive.'" University of Waikato History Web page. [Online] http://www.waikato.ac.nz/wfass/subjects/history/waimilhist/1999/foch.htm (accessed May 2001).

"Foch, Ferdinand." *DiscoverySchool.com.* [Online] http://school.discovery.com/homeworkhelp/worldbook/atozhistory/f/sa202580.html (accessed May 2001).

Douglas Haig

June 19, 1861
Edinburgh, Scotland
January 30, 1928
London, England

Soldier, general, commander of British army

When World War I began, Douglas Haig was widely considered to be Britain's greatest soldier. However by war's end, Haig was just as widely considered a butcher, a distant leader who had sent hundreds of thousands of British youth to their deaths. Although the public view of Douglas Haig had been altered, Haig himself had not changed. From the start of his career he was entirely devoted to the principles of duty, honor, and hard work. These principles lay behind the orders he gave to the thousands of British soldiers who fought on the terrible battlefields of Ypres and the Somme. But these principles and Haig's outdated military methods both failed in the battles of World War I. Haig's fall from glory was a signal that the world had been changed forever by World War I, and that the old ideas of glory and honor were no longer as important as they had been in the past.

An Unlikely Soldier

Little in Douglas Haig's early life indicated that he would become a great soldier. Born on June 19, 1861, Haig was one of nine children. His family was quite wealthy: His father,

John, ran a family-owned whiskey distillery, and his mother, Rachel, came from a rich family. Haig did not distinguish himself early in life, being a mediocre student at Clifton College (the equivalent of a private high school in the United States). Haig went on to Oxford University in 1880. There he improved his skills as a horseman and a polo player, but he still struggled as a student.

Even though he showed no previous interest in the military, Haig took the unusual step of enrolling at the British Royal Military College at Sandhurst (often called simply Sandhurst) after leaving Oxford. Biographers speculate that the military college may have offered the best chance for developing his skills as a horseman. At Sandhurst, however, Haig found his calling. Avoiding the social life of the college, Haig worked diligently and rose to the top of his class. It was said that he made up for his lack of intellect with his powers of concentration and dedication to his work. By his last year at Sandhurst he had become senior underofficer, the highest student office in the school. According to Gene Smith in *The Ends of Greatness*, an instructor wrote this of Haig: "A Scottish lad, Douglas Haig, is tops in almost everything, books, drill, riding and sports; he is to go into the cavalry and before he is finished he will be top of the army."

A Soldier of the Empire

In the cavalry (troops trained to fight on horseback) Haig was an officer. His first assignment was with the prestigious Seventh Hussars. He distinguished himself first on the polo field, where he led his new regiment to several trophies. But Haig began soldiering in earnest in 1886, when he was transferred to India, which was then under British control. In India Haig alternated between staff posts—where he learned about communications, administration, and transportation—and cavalry commands—where he mastered the tactics of mounted warfare. By 1896 Haig was accepted into Staff College, the training academy for the finest British officers. At the academy Haig learned about strategy, tactics, and other elements of warfare. As at Sandhurst, Haig stood out from the other officers both for his refusal to become involved in social affairs and for his dedication to work.

All Haig needed to prove himself as a soldier was experience in actual combat. In 1898 he got his chance when he was sent to Egypt to help suppress a native rebellion in Sudan, just south of Egypt. For ten months Haig fought in the desert, conducting himself well in the battles of Omdurman and the battle of Atbara. Once the rebellion was crushed, Haig was sent to Great Britain's South African territories to fight against the descendants of Dutch settlers (Boers) in what became known as the Boer War (1899–1902). Haig again served with honor and won the rank of colonel.

From 1902 to 1914 Haig bounced back and forth from India to England, all the while progressing in rank. In 1906 he took command of the imperial general staff and was responsible for overseeing the training and organization of troops serving in British colonies all over the world. In 1907 Haig published his only book, *Cavalry Studies, Strategical and Tactical,* in which he outlined his belief in the continuing importance of cavalry attacks in modern war. In 1912 he obtained the post of director of military training at the British War Office, where he was second in command to war secretary Richard Haldane. The pair had two goals: to reorganize the British armed forces for fighting in distant colonies and to prepare another force for what seemed like an inevitable war on the continent of Europe. Thus they organized the British Expeditionary Force, a highly trained army of soldiers who could be quickly assembled to fight on foreign soil. In addition to his steady rise in the British military, Haig experienced personal satisfaction: In 1905 he met and married Dorothy Vivian, a maid of honor to the queen.

The Ultimate Test: World War I

On August 4, 1914, the British Expeditionary Force (BEF) that Haig and Haldane had created was called into service. Following the assassination of an Austrian archduke, Germany and Austria-Hungary had lined up against France, Russia, and then Great Britain in a conflict to see who would dominate Europe. Field Marshal John French (1852–1925) was placed in command of the BEF, which consisted of two corps; Haig was in charge of one of those corps and reported to French. French ordered the entire BEF to France to fight the Germans; Haig protested that this would leave no one in Britain to train the soldiers that would be needed for future battles. French, believing his forces would quickly defeat the

Germans, overruled Haig and sent the entire force. It soon proved a costly decision.

Haig and his troops—some forty thousand men—faced the enemy near Mons, Belgium, on August 23, 1914, and the Germans' huge advantage in numbers of soldiers soon took its toll. The French armies fell back in retreat, and John French soon ordered his men to retreat as well. Haig led his retreating troops west and slightly north, trying desperately to keep German troops from flanking them. (To be flanked, or attacked from the side, was deadly in battle.) By late fall of 1914 Haig and the British finally succeeded at stopping the Germans, in what became known as the first battle of Ypres. French's leadership had nearly destroyed the original BEF and left the British army in a stalemate of trench warfare with the Germans along the Western Front (the area along France and Germany where fighting took place). By late 1915 British politicians relieved French of his command and appointed Haig as the new leader.

Douglas Haig (third from left) visiting troops during World War I. Haig served in India and was then given command of the First Army Corps of the British Expeditionary Force in France and Belgium when hostilities began in 1914. *Reproduced by permission of Hulton Getty/Archive Photos, Inc.*

In Command: The Tragedy of the Somme and Passchendaele

As Haig inspected his command, he saw little use for the cavalry that he had so diligently prepared for in his years of studying the art of war. Cavalry were useless in trench warfare; powerful machine guns sped the pace at which men were killed; and his army was now filled with raw recruits rather than trained and experienced soldiers. But Haig thought he saw a way to defeat the Germans in 1916. He would launch a massive assault near the Somme River. Late in June 1916, the British began a sustained artillery bombardment of the German forces along the Somme. For seven days and seven nights, the bombs fell on German positions, and on July 1 British troops rose out of their trenches and marched forward into the most terrific slaughter yet seen in the history of war (see sidebar).

Despite the massive cost in British lives in the battle of the Somme, Haig was promoted from general to field marshal on January 1, 1916, and he faced the next year of battle even more determined to defeat the Germans with the tactics he had used on the Somme. He planned his next attack on the northern end of the Western Front, near the Belgian town of Passchendaele. The battle of Passchendaele mirrored that of the Somme: days of bombardment, followed with a mass assault by armed men. Haig believed that his plan would work this time, for his bombing was more accurate, his men were better trained, and the enemy defenses were not as strong. Sadly, he was wrong. German defenses had improved, and their machinegun nests survived the bombardment. Worse, days of rain turned the fields of Passchendaele into a vast sea of mud. Though the British soldiers dutifully rose from the trenches on July 31 to attack the Germans, they soon found themselves stuck in craters of mud, unable to move and pounded by machinegun fire.

Unwilling to give up his offensive, Haig ordered his men to continue the attack. For weeks and weeks British soldiers died miserably in the mud fields of Passchendaele. By November 10 the British had lost nearly 250,000 soldiers and had gained just 4 miles of territory. Haig called it a victory, but civilian leaders did not agree. British prime minister David Lloyd George (1863–1945) was appalled at the loss of life at the Somme and Passchendaele, and he implored Haig to try new methods. But Haig could see no other way out of the war; he

The battle of the Somme

Beginning on June 23, 1916, the British launched the most sustained artillery attack of the war, targeting German positions near the Somme River. The bombardment could be heard all the way to England. British General Douglas Haig believed that such shelling would thoroughly destroy the German trench system and that his young soldiers would only have to march forward to claim victory. The soldiers had been told, according to a source quoted by Jay Winter and Blain Baggett in *The Great War and the Shaping of the Twentieth Century,* "You will be able to go over the top with a walking stick, you will not need rifles. You will find the Germans all dead, not even a rat will have survived." But that was not what they found at all. Despite all the bombing, well-fortified German trench positions had held firm. As the British soldiers climbed out of their trenches, the Germans raked them with machinegun fire. By the end of that first day's attack, twenty thousand British soldiers had been killed and forty thousand wounded. Several brigades lost a majority of their men; the fourteenth platoon of the First Rifle Brigade lost thirty-nine of forty

men. It was the beginning of a true military disaster.

Because of poor communications, Haig didn't realize the toll the first day of battle had taken on British troops. He ordered the men to battle on. For days the British threw themselves against the German line. On July 14 they got through the second German line, only to be turned back by fresh German reserves. The battle soon turned into a test of wills, as generals on both sides threw men into the killing fields for months on end. Through August and September and into the fall, British and German troops took turns trying to break each other. Neither side succeeded.

Weather and fatigue brought the battle of the Somme to a close at the end of November. The British had succeeded in advancing six miles and claiming the village of BeaumontHamel, but they had lost 420,000 soldiers in this battle alone, followed by 195,000 for the French. The Germans sustained a total of 650,000 casualties. Because they had gained a small bit of territory, the Allies declared themselves the winners.

told Lloyd George that Great Britain must simply try again in 1918. Lloyd George could not fire Haig—there were no suitable generals to take Haig's place—so he did the only thing he could do to prevent more casualties: He refused to send more men into Haig's killing machine. Haig would have to fight in 1918 with the men he had available.

Haig's Triumph and Decline

The Germans, too, had been sorely tested by their battles with the British and the French on the Western Front. In the spring of 1918 Germany decided to launch one last, desperate offensive to try to win the war. Across the Western Front the Germans pushed forward, and they gained more ground than either side had gained since the very first days of the war. But the British and the French fought well in retreat, cheered on by Haig's famous "backs-to-the-wall" message, in which he states: "Many amongst us now are tired. To those I would say that Victory will belong to the side which holds out the longest. There must be no retirement. With our backs to the wall and believing in the justice of our cause each one must fight on to the end." When joined by the American troops, the Allies were able to halt the German advance by July 1918. The German army, nearing collapse, quickly fell to Allied attacks through the summer and fall of 1918, and on November 11, 1918, the war ended with the Germans soundly defeated.

Had Haig returned to Great Britain immediately after the end of the war, he might have been greeted as a hero. After all, he was the military commander of victorious troops. But Haig stayed in Europe for nearly six months, overseeing the needs of British troops there; and by the time he returned, many British citizens and politicians had begun to question the wisdom of sending so many of Britain's young men to such an early grave. Haig was granted a title upon his return—he became earl of Bemersyde—and he lived out his postwar years in comfort in Scotland. But he was far from a national hero. In fact, many labeled Haig the architect of World War I's terrible slaughter. Critics said that Haig fought a modern war with old-fashioned methods, that he cared nothing for the lives of his soldiers, that he was a butcher, callous and cruel. They claimed that he was a relic from the past and that men would never again naively march off to die for the glory of their country.

Haig, who had never been one to argue or try to shape public opinion, watched in silence as his reputation plummeted. On January 28, 1928, just two days before his death, he gave a speech to a group of Boy Scouts. His advice, quoted in Smith's *The Ends of Greatness*, was this: "When you grow up, always remember that you belong to a great empire, and when people speak disrespectfully of England always stand up and defend your country."

For More Information

Books

Smith, Gene. *The Ends of Greatness: Haig, Pétain, Rathenau, and Eden; Victims of History.* New York: Crown Publishers, 1990.

Terraine, John. *Douglas Haig: The Educated Soldier.* London: L. Cooper, 1990.

Warner, Philip. *Field Marshal Earl Haig.* London: Bodley Head, 1991.

Winter, Denis. *Haig's Command: A Reassessment.* London and New York: Viking, 1991.

Winter, Jay, and Blain Baggett. *The Great War and the Shaping of the Twentieth Century.* New York: Penguin Studio, 1996.

Articles

Atwater, James D. "Echoes and Voices Summoned from a Half-Hour in Hell." *Smithsonian,* November 1987.

Web sites

"Douglas Haig." *Teaching History Online.* [Online] http://www.spartacus.schoolnet.co.uk/FWWhaig.htm (accessed May 2001).

"First Earl Douglas Haig." *Trenches on the Web.* [Online] http://worldwar1.com/biochaig.htm (accessed May 2001).

Jean Jaurès

September 3, 1859
Castres, France
July 31, 1914
Paris, France

Teacher, journalist, political leader

"Courage means to search for the truth and to tell it, to refuse to let the law be buried under the passing triumphant lie, and to refuse to echo the applause of fools or the cries of fanatics."

—*Jean Jaurès, July 1903.*

Jean Jaurès. *Photograph courtesy of The Library of Congress.*

Though his life was cut short by an assassin's bullet, Jean Jaurès made a lasting contribution to French politics. A brilliant teacher, writer, and political thinker, Jaurès was most importantly an idealist who believed that society's hope lay not in fighting or struggle but in the free thoughts and dreams of its working people. Perhaps the greatest testimony to Jaurès's enduring contribution is that dozens of schools all over France have been named after him. A strong supporter of freedom and excellence in education for all, Jaurès might have been proudest of this legacy.

A Passion for Learning

Jaurès was born to lower-middle-class parents on September 3, 1859, in Castres, a small textile center in the southwest of France. A quick and enthusiastic student, he was anxious to get the best education possible, so he left his home as soon as he could to continue his studies in Paris. However, he always had an affection for the area he came from and returned there to work at different times throughout his life.

In 1879 at the age of twenty, Jaurès entered the École Normale Supérieure, a respected college in Paris. Three years later, he graduated with a degree in philosophy and moved to Albi, near his hometown, to teach high school. In 1883, he went to teach at the University of Toulouse, also in the south of France. In 1885, he was elected to the Chamber of Deputies, the most important lawmaking body of France at that time. He enjoyed politics, and though he was defeated in the 1889 election, he ran again in 1893 and was elected once more.

As a young deputy, Jaurès did not forget his experiences as a student and a teacher. He strongly recommended that more towns create good schools for the working people who lived there. He believed in the separation of church and state, and he thought it was important that these schools be secular, or nonreligious. He insisted that students needed to be exposed to ideas, thoughts, and experiences beyond those that they had grown up with. He also defended the right of students to express themselves and learn to think for themselves.

Socialism and Activism

It was during his second term as a deputy that Jaurès began to embrace the ideas of socialism. Socialism is a political and economic theory based on the idea of cooperation and shared resources for the common good. The idea of socialism originated in Europe during the eighteenth and early nineteenth centuries. This was the time of the Industrial Revolution, when the discovery of electricity and the invention of the steam engine and other machines led to the construction of factories. Goods that had once been made by hand at home or in craft shops were now manufactured in large quantities by workers running machines. The factories brought great wealth to their owners, but those who worked in the factories were often poor, mistreated, and underpaid. As these injustices became obvious, many people began to think that there must be a way to divide the profits from the new industries so that the workers themselves could benefit more from their own labor. Some of the first socialist thinkers were French, including François-Nöl Babeuf and the count of Saint-Simon, Claude Henri de Rouvroy. There also were many other important socialists all over Europe, such as Karl Marx of Germany and Charles Kingsley of England.

Left, Right, and Center: The Political Dance

Journalists and others who write and talk about politics often use the terms "right" and "left" to describe different political views. Those on the right tend to be more conservative; that is, they are in favor of little change or very slow change in the way things are. Conservatives usually support traditional ways of thinking—they are often identified as the "old guard" or the "establishment," meaning that they approve of the political system that already exists. Those on the left work for change in the existing political system. Leftists are also called liberals. Liberals are in favor of change and reform in society, with the goal of improving people's lives. On the right, people are more likely to be unquestioningly loyal to their country; those on the left more frequently challenge their country's actions and policies.

Those on the extreme right are called reactionaries. Rather than resisting changes, as conservatives do, reactionaries want things to change back to how they used to be. Those on the extreme left are called radicals. Radicals do not favor the slow, steady progress that the liberals work toward. Instead, they think that society needs big changes quickly. Both radicals and reactionaries sometimes support violent revolution to achieve their goals. The Nazi Party which rose to power in Germany in 1933 is an example of an extreme right-wing party. The Communist Party which dominated Russia until 1991 is an example of an extreme left-wing party.

The Dictionary of Word and Phrase Origins, edited by William and Mary Morris (New York: Harper and Row, 1988), suggests that these terms came into use because of the habit in European legislatures of seating the conservative parties on the right of the king or prime minister and the liberal parties on the left. Being seated on the right of an important person is traditionally a sign of rank and favor, and the conservatives, who generally supported those in power, were given that favor. The liberals, who might be working to change the balance of power, were seated less favorably on the left.

Jaurès had been raised in a district of textile mills and mines, and he read about the struggles of the factory workers and miners from his hometown who were fighting for better conditions by forming unions and going on strike. As he learned more about the struggle of working people, he became more and more interested in the ideas of socialism. He developed his own theories and began to write and speak about them. He founded several socialist newspapers, including *L'Humanité* (*Humanity*) in 1904. While some socialists called for a class war, insisting that the workers must rise up and take control by force, Jaurès had a vision of a democratic socialism, the belief that the middle class and the working class could work together to create a fair division of power. He hoped that the rise of socialism could be a peaceful transformation based on a positive vision of what society could be.

In 1894 Alfred Dreyfus (1859–1935), a French army officer of Jewish descent, was accused of treason, convicted, and condemned to life in prison. At that time, those of high rank in the French army and government were mainly Catholic, and many of them were anti-Jewish. Many socialists and others on the left thought that Dreyfus had been framed because he was Jewish. Jaurès was one of Dreyfus's most outspoken defenders, and he wrote articles about the incident for socialist newspapers. Though Dreyfus was eventually pardoned, the "Dreyfus Affair," as it was called, tore French society apart, with the "Dreyfusards" on the left and the "anti-Dreyfusards" on the right. ("Left" and "right" are terms referring to a person's political views. A person on the left is willing to accept political change, while a person on the right does not support change.) Jaurès lost his seat in the Chamber of Deputies in 1889 because of his public support of Dreyfus. However, in 1902 Jaurès was once again elected to serve as a deputy, and he remained part of the chamber until his death.

One positive result of the Dreyfus Affair was that it united the many different socialist groups around a single cause; all of these groups were angered at the poor treatment of an outsider at the hands of the ruling interests. Jaurès had long hoped and worked for such unity, and in 1905 he helped form the French Socialist Party, which joined the major socialist parties into one unified group.

Peace Activist

After the assassination of Archduke Franz Ferdinand on June 28, 1914, Jaurès began to speak out against the alliances that entangled France. He was mistrustful of the Russians and the British, with whom France had treaties, and he even thought that an alliance with the Germans (whom many French people hated) made more sense. Most of all, Jaurès dis-

Jean Jaurès speaking during a protest rally. Jaurès spoke out against the war since he believed that socialism, not fighting, could bring world peace. *Reproduced by permission of Archive Photos, Inc.*

liked nationalism (devotion to the interests of a particular nation) and the wars it so often produced. He was in favor of negotiation between nations rather than fighting. So, as the countries of Europe began declaring war on one another, Jaurès began to speak out against the war and against France's allies. He suggested that socialism could bring world peace and that France should not join in the war.

His speeches and writings angered French people who supported the war and who were motivated by strong patriotic feelings, especially those people who hated the socialist ideas that Jaurès supported. On July 31, 1914, three days before France entered World War I, Jaurès was assassinated as he sat at a café in Paris. His killer, Raoul Villain, has been described by many as a fanatic patriot who was angered by Jaurès's speeches against the war.

Besides being a powerful speaker, Jaurès was a productive writer who started several newspapers and wrote many books. Among his works are *Action Socialiste* (*Socialist Action*; 1899), *Études Socialistes* (*Socialist Studies*; 1901), and *Histoire Socialiste de la Révolution Française, 1789–1900* (*Socialist History of the French Revolution, 1789–1900*; 1901–08), an eight-volume study of the French Revolution.

For More Information

Books

Goldberg, Harvey. *The Life of Jean Jaurès.* Madison: University of Wisconsin Press, 1962.

Jackson, J. Hampden. *Jean Jaurès, His Life and Work.* London: G. Allen and Unwin, 1943.

Weinstein, Harold R. *Jean Jaurès: A Story of Patriotism in the French Socialist Movement.* New York: Columbia University Press, 1936.

Williams, Stuart, ed. *Socialism in France: From Jaurès to Mitterrand.* New York: St. Martin's Press, 1983.

Web sites

Gianoulis, Tina, Translator. "Jean Jaurès, July 1903." [Online] http://www.ukans.edu/~kansite/wwi0300/msg00150.html (accessed April 2001).

Käthe Kollwitz

July 8, 1867
Königsberg, East Prussia
April 22, 1945
Moritzburg, Germany

Artist, humanitarian

"This woman of manly heart has looked on [the poor], has taken them into her motherly arms with a solemn and tender compassion. She is the voice for the silence of those who have been sacrificed."

—*Romain Rolland, winner of the 1915 Nobel Prize in Literature, in Mina C. and Arthur H. Klein,* Käthe Kollwitz: Life in Art,

Käthe Kollwitz. *Reproduced by permission of Corbis-Bettmann.*

During a career that lasted more than sixty years, Prussian-born Käthe Kollwitz created a large number of prints and drawings that earned her a reputation as one of the most important graphic artists of her era. Some of her works depict the impact of World War I on women and children and make a powerful statement about the horror of the war. Kollwitz was the daughter of liberal parents who instilled in her a lifelong hatred of militarism (the buildup of military power by governments) and social injustice. Kollwitz created works that reflected her concern for the oppressed, especially the suffering people in her own country. Among her earliest and most famous works was a series of prints titled *A Weavers' Uprising,* (1897) inspired by German writer Gerhart Hauptmann's drama about striking textile workers in Silesia (an industrial region in present-day Poland).

Kollwitz earned the nickname "The Socialist Artist" for her strongly expressive prints that depicted life from the point of view of the downtrodden. After her brother was killed in combat during World War I, her works often incorporated themes of death and melancholy—an expression of her profound sadness at the horror of war—and she began allying herself with some of Germany's leftist groups. These political groups supported socialist programs that would protect the interests of the common people, as opposed to the interests of businesses and wealthy people. After the Nazis (a German political party led by Adolf Hitler that promoted racism and the expansion of state power) came to power in the 1930s, Kollwitz's works were declared "degenerate," or politically unacceptable, and she was forbidden to teach or display her art. Although she didn't leave the country, she was deeply distressed by the rise of anti-Semitism (hatred of Jews) in Germany during the 1930s and early 1940s. She died in April 1945, a few weeks before the end of World War II (1939–45).

Reared a Radical

Käthe Kollwitz was born Käthe Ida Schmidt in Königsberg, East Prussia, on July 8, 1867. She was the daughter of Karl Schmidt, a master mason (stonecutter) who had once studied law, and his wife Katharina Rupp, a cultivated woman who enjoyed reading both German and English literature. Käthe was the fifth of seven children, three of whom died in infancy. The surviving children included an older brother and two sisters, one older and one younger than Käthe. Käthe's maternal grandfather, Julius Rupp, the spiritual leader of a liberal and nonconformist (a person not complying with established church rules) Protestant congregation, had been sympathetic to the leftist revolutionaries who tried to overthrow the kaiser's rule in 1848. (The Kaiser was the emperor of Prussia.) Rupp later served in the Prussian legislature but was imprisoned in the 1850s for his political activities. Young Käthe was thus brought up in a radical household—one that identified with the underdog and supported progressive causes. When Rupp retired from his ministry, he was succeeded by his son-in-law Karl Schmidt, Käthe's father.

As an adolescent Käthe often exhibited periods of depression and nervousness. She was schooled at home because her parents objected to the conservative Prussian state school system. Käthe had an obvious talent for drawing, and when she was sixteen, she started taking formal art lessons from Rudolph Mauer, an engraver, who taught her how to draw and make etchings and prints. From an early age, Käthe chose poor and working people as subjects for her art, preferring to draw pictures of dockworkers or weavers instead of landscapes or still lifes (pictures of nonliving objects). She also enjoyed reading the poetry of Friedrich Schiller (1759–1805) and the plays of dramatist Johann Wolfgang von Goethe (1749–1832), who remained an important influence on her to the end of her life, even though his political views were more conservative than her own. Käthe's elder brother, Konrad, introduced her to the writings of more radical European writers, like Émile Zola and Henrik Ibsen, and also the Russian naturalists, such as Leo Tolstoy, Fyodor Dostoyevsky, and Maksim Gorky. While living in London, England, Konrad made the acquaintance of socialist thinker Friedrich Engels (1820–1895), who had collaborated with Karl Marx (1818–1883) in creating the theoretical base for modern communism. (Both socialism and communism are political systems that advocate shared or government ownership of the production and ownership of goods.) Besides passing on his political enthusiasm to Käthe, Konrad also introduced her to his friend, Karl Kollwitz, a socialist and medical student. In 1884 Käthe and Karl became engaged.

Painting Life as It Really Was

The same year that Käthe became engaged, she traveled to Berlin and Munich with her mother and her sister Lise. In Berlin, she met her sister's friend Gerhart Hauptmann, author of *The Weavers,* a play that protested the working conditions in the textile mills of Silesia. Käthe would later make a series of highly acclaimed prints that were inspired by Hauptmann's writing. Soon afterwards, she enrolled in the School for Women Artists in Berlin, where her principal instructor was Karl Stauffer-Bern, a Swiss artist. He introduced Käthe to the work of his friend Max Klinger, a painter and sculptor of the naturalist school. (The naturalists created works that tried to show life as it really was, with all its blemishes, unlike the impressionists, who used light and color techniques to mask the gritty realities of the scenes they portrayed.) Max Klinger's work was to have a profound influence on Käthe's developing style.

After a year in Berlin, Käthe returned to Königsberg to study privately. There, her interest in portraying ordinary working people and unromantic situations deepened. In 1888 she moved to Munich, which was then a very important center of artistic activity in Europe. She studied at the School for Women Artists under Ludwig Hertereich, a painter, but she made a decisive move to graphics, or printmaking. During this period, she perfected the techniques of etching that would bring her recognition as one of the finest graphic artists of her generation.

In 1891, Käthe married Karl Kollwitz, who was by then a practicing physician; he worked with working-class patients in a poor neighborhood in Berlin. Their first child, Hans, was born the following year and their second son, Peter, in 1896. Although Karl did not earn much money, he supported his wife's artistic ambitions. Käthe Kollwitz had little success in exhibiting her works in galleries dominated by more traditional artists, but in 1893 she became a part of a group of radical young artists that broke away from the more conservative Association of Berlin Artists. When Hauptmann's play *The Weavers* was staged in Berlin that year, Kollwitz was inspired to create a cycle of prints called *A Weavers' Uprising.* These prints portrayed textile workers being exploited by capitalist bosses (people who privately own the means of production and the distribution of goods), rising up in protest, and being brought under control by the Prussian military. When the prints were exhibited, an art jury wanted to award Kollwitz a gold medal. However, the prize was blocked by Kaiser Wilhelm II, who like many other rulers did not want to see artists portraying contemporary social conditions. Later, the kaiserin (kaiser's wife) refused to attend an exhibit in Berlin until Kollwitz's works were removed. In spite of such official criticism, Kollwitz's prints won gold medals in international competitions and were added to the collections of the Dresden Museum and other prestigious art institutions.

Success as an Artist

Kollwitz soon gained an international reputation for the quality of her work. She became an instructor in graphics and figure drawing at the Berlin School for Women Artists, where she encouraged her students to bypass the traditional method of imitating old masters and develop their imaginations and creativity instead. Kollwitz continued to find inspiration in the struggles of common folk, creating the *Peasants' War,* a series of prints made between 1902 and 1908 and inspired by the sixteenth-century farmers' uprisings that occurred across central Europe.

In 1904, Kollwitz visited Paris, France, for several weeks and adopted a poor boy named Georg Gretor, the son of one of her former Munich classmates. In 1907, she won a prize that enabled her to spend a year in Florence, Italy. During her stay there, she met a twenty-year-old free-spirited English-woman named Constanza Harding, who wore her hair mannishly short, carried a revolver, and preferred to be known as "Stan." Kollwitz and Stan became fast friends and set off on a threehundred-mile walking trip to Rome before rejoining Kollwitz's husband and younger son, who had come from Berlin. After her trips abroad, Kollwitz's subject matter and medium (type of artwork) shifted somewhat: Instead of concentrating on class struggle, she began focusing on mothers and their children; and she began experimenting with sculpture, though she remained primarily a printmaker. Her visit to Italy had familiarized her with the theme of Madonna and Child and the Pietà (a representation of the Virgin Mary holding the dead Christ), and as late as the 1930s Kollwitz was creating sculptures inspired by these themes.

The Impact of World War I

In 1912, Kollwitz traveled to New York for the first exhibition of her works in the United States. Two years later, World War I broke out, and Kollwitz's beloved younger son, Peter, was killed in Belgium that October. Profoundly grief-stricken, Kollwitz planned a memorial sculpture called *Mourning Parents* that she wanted to dedicate to the mothers and fathers of all who died in battle; it was finally completed in 1931 and placed in a veterans' cemetery in Roggevelde, Belgium. The sculpture—one of the best-known artistic works to commemorate the war—depicts a mother and father kneeling in grief amidst row after row of wooden crosses; the grieving parents bear the features of Kollwitz and her husband. In the 1950s, both the cemetery and the sculpture were moved to a new site at Vladsloo-Praebosch.

During and after World War I, Kollwitz created many sculptures and prints that depicted the horrible wasting of young lives on the battlefields of Europe. Among the more famous of these are the drawings *Widows and Orphans* (1919),

Killed in Action (1921), and *Survivors* (1923). Kollwitz refused to join other German artists and intellectuals in their appeals to German patriotism. Instead, she became increasingly pacifist (opposed to conflict and war), and in a letter published in socialist newspapers she criticized militarism and nationalism (devotion to national interests and independence), closing with these words: "There has been enough of dying! Let not another man fall! . . . Seed for the planting shall not be ground up!"

After World War I ended, Kollwitz became the first woman elected to the Prussian Academy of Arts and, against her wishes, received the title of professor. In 1928, she became the supervisor of master graphic students at that institution. In the years of disillusionment that followed Germany's defeat in World War I, Kollwitz supported the socialist and communist causes and created posters advocating assistance for the newly established Soviet Union. However, she insisted that her work was not political and that she was creating it as an artist and as a humanitarian. During the 1920s, she devoted herself to a series of woodblock prints called *War* that graphically depict the sufferings of women and children during the conflict. She believed that if her art had any purpose, it was in the service of pacifism—to support and inspire those who were working to eliminate war around the world.

Clashing with the Nazis

In the 1930s, Kollwitz spoke out against the rise of Nazism. The Nazis tried to purge German art of what they considered leftist influences. When Kollwitz's work became the target of some pro-Nazi critics, she lent her support to the Society of Revolutionary Artists and defiantly continued to create posters that sympathized with the class struggle, as well as tender portrayals of mothers and children. Many of her pictures were exhibited in the Soviet Union during this period, to great acclaim.

Because of her anti-Nazi stand, Kollwitz was forced to resign from the Prussian Academy and was forbidden to teach, though she continued to do so privately. Her husband also was harassed by the government. In spite of these pressures, including a visit from the Gestapo (German security police known for terrorizing German citizens), Kollwitz steadfastly refused to change her artistic vision to suit the Nazi government. In 1937, many of her prints and drawings were removed from museums and art galleries by the Nazi government. The Nazis burned books and artwork, including Kollwitz's that they found objectionable. Kollwitz's work was exhibited in New York, Los Angeles, and other foreign cities, but never again in her homeland during her lifetime. Undaunted, she wrote in a letter, "For Germany I am dead, but for America I have begun to come alive. That is wonderful!"

It was during these difficult days that Kollwitz began work on her last great graphics project, a series of lithographs titled *Death.* The eight prints in the series bear such titles as *Death Reaches into a Group of Children, Woman Entrusts Herself to Death,* and *Death Seizes a Woman.* Kollwitz created a number of bronze sculptures—including *Soldiers' Wives Waving Good-Bye* and *Tower of Mothers*—depicting the extreme sadness of mothers seeing their children suffering under unjust and militaristic regimes. She also created memorial sculptures for the graves of Jewish friends who had been persecuted by the Nazis. Just before her husband died in 1940, she created *Farewell,* a tiny bronze sculpture that depicts a woman embracing a man who seems to be moving into another dimension.

Kollwitz remained in Berlin during the early part of World War II. Her last great lithograph, completed in 1942, shows a defiant woman protecting small children with her massive arms. It is titled *Seed for the Planting Shall Not Be Ground Up,* the line from one of Goethe's poems that she used to conclude her antiwar letter a quarter-century earlier. That September, Kollwitz's grandson, Peter, had been killed in combat in Russia. The following year, Kollwitz fled Berlin to live in Nordhausen with a young sculptor friend, Margaret Böning. Shortly after Kollwitz left, her Berlin home and many of her works were destroyed in an air raid. A memorial park named in her honor now graces the site.

In 1943, a sickly Kollwitz accepted the offer of an admirer and collector, Prince Ernst Heinrich of Saxony, to take refuge at his estate in Moritzburg, near Dresden, where she lived out her remaining days surrounded by books written by Goethe. She died there on April 22, 1945, just a week before Hitler's own death. Her ashes were later buried in the family's plot at Friedrichsfelde cemetery in Berlin.

For More Information

Books

Cornebise, Alfred E. *Art from the Trenches: America's Uniformed Artists in World War I.* College Station: Texas A & M University Press, 1991.

Gallatin, A. E. *Art and the Great War.* New York: E. P. Dutton, 1919.

Kearns, Martha. *Käthe Kollwitz: Woman and Artist.* Old Westbury, NY: The Feminist Press, 1976.

Klein, Mina C., and H. Arthur. *Käthe Kollwitz: Life in Art*. New York: Holt, Rinehart and Winston, 1972.

Web sites

Art of the First World War. [Online] http://www.artww1.com/gb/index2.html (accessed April 2001).

"Fractal Gallery." *Trenches on the Web*. [Online] http://www.worldwar1.com/fracgal.htm (accessed April 2001).

"Käthe Kollwitz." *Artcyclopedia*. [Online] http://www.artcyclopedia.com/artists/kollwitz_kathe.html (accessed March 2001).

"KätheKollwitzMuseum, Berlin." [Online] http://www.kaethekollwitzde (accessed March 2001).

Fritz Kreisler

February 2, 1875
Vienna, Austria
January 29, 1962
New York City, New York

Violinist

The Austrian-born musician Fritz Kreisler was the world's leading violinist in the first decades of the twentieth century. He became especially popular with U.S. audiences in 1888 after his Boston and New York debuts as a twelve-year-old prodigy (a highly talented child). When World War I broke out in 1914, he served briefly in the Austrian army and was wounded in combat against the Russians. He was on a U.S. concert tour in 1917 when the United States entered World War I on the side of the Allies, which was composed of France, Great Britain, Russia, and later the United States. Because of Kreisler's previous war service, he was branded an "enemy alien" by many American patriotic and civic organizations. As public prejudice grew against him, first Pittsburgh and then other U.S. cities banned his performances, and he was forced to abandon his concert tour.

After the war, Kreisler was eventually welcomed back to American concert halls, and he firmly reestablished his reputation as a violin virtuoso (a highly skilled musician). Though he lived in Berlin, Germany, he made many concert tours abroad. In 1938, after Germany annexed his native Austria,

"As an Austrian and as a soldier, I owe every drop of my blood, every dollar that I can earn, to my country; but as an artist I am above all politics and owe my best to the world."

—*Fritz Kreisler, quoted in Amy Biancolli,* Fritz Kreisler: Love's Sorrow, Love's Joy, *p.108.*

Fritz Kreisler. *Reproduced by permission of HultonDeutsch Collection/CorbisBettmann.*

Kreisler was drafted into the German army. In order not serve in the army, however, he became a French citizen the following year and fled with his wife to the United States, where they lived for the rest of their lives. He became a U.S. citizen in 1943. His final public performance took place in 1950, when he appeared on the "Bell Telephone Hour" radio program. Kreisler died in New York City on January 29, 1962, a few days before his eighty-seventh birthday.

A Child Prodigy

Fritz Kreisler was born in Vienna, Austria, on February 2, 1875, the second of five children born to Salomon Severin Kreisler, a Polish-born physician and amateur violinist, and his wife, Anna. Like many other middle-class households in Vienna during that period, the Kreislers were educated and cosmopolitan (interested in culture and new ideas), and music played an important role in their family life. The young psychoanalyst (a person who treats psychic disorders) Sigmund Freud (1856–1939) was among the friends who played violin at the informal musical parties that the Kreislers hosted. As a boy, Kreisler thrived in this musical environment. Taught by his father, he started playing on a toy violin when he was four years old and quickly proved himself a prodigy. At age seven, Kreisler became the youngest pupil ever admitted to the Vienna Conservatory, a prominent music school. His principal teacher was Joseph Hellmesberger Jr., but Kreisler also studied composition with the noted composer Anton Bruckner (1824–1896) and also played informal duets with Johannes Brahms (1833–1897) after becoming acquainted with him at a local musicians' club. Despite his musical genius, Kreisler hated practicing. Still, he progressed rapidly, and by age ten he won a gold medal for his violin playing. In 1885, he left Vienna to enroll in the Paris Conservatory of Music, where he competed against adult students to win the conservatory's highest prize.

In 1888, the twelve-year-old Kreisler made his U.S. debut in a fifty-concert tour with pianist Moriz Rosenthal (1862– 1946), playing first in Boston, then in New York, Chicago, St. Louis, and other major cities. One New York critic described Kreisler's playing as "charming, if not astonishing." Returning to Vienna the following year, Kreisler decided to quit the violin and finish his formal education at the Piaritsen Gymnasium (a German high school). He then decided to follow his father's profession and entered medical school at the University of Vienna. However, Kreisler fantasized about living a life that included being a surgeon in the morning, a chess player in the afternoon, a violinist in the evening, and a victorious soldier at midnight. He quit medical school after two years and enlisted as a soldier in the Austrian imperial army; he served as the violin accompanist to Archduke Eugene, the grandnephew of Emperor Franz Josef (1830–1916). It was during this period of military service that Kreisler decided to devote his life's energies to the violin. In 1896, a civilian once more, he took up the instrument again, and by the turn of the century he had made his debuts with the Vienna and the Berlin Philharmonics. He also began composing arrangements for violin, some of which were later published. However, he later confessed that some of the compositions he had claimed to be his own were actually written by other famous composers.

While sailing back to Europe after an American tour in 1901, Kreisler met Harriet Lies, a New York-born divorcée who was the daughter of a German American tobacco merchant. They fell in love immediately and were married a year later, though they repeated the ceremony three more times because of legal technicalities.

In 1910, the Victor Phonograph Company signed Kreisler to an exclusive contract, making him one of the first musicians to have his performances captured in the new medium of sound recordings. He was the first classical violinist to have his performances widely disseminated via recordings, and as a result, his talents became widely known to audiences who were unable to attend live performances.

Victim of Wartime Hysteria

When World War I broke out in the summer of 1914, Kreisler was drafted into the Austrian army, and just four weeks later he was wounded in combat against Russian troops. Honorably discharged from the service, he quickly recovered from his wounds and soon left for the United States, where he performed at New York's Carnegie Hall in November. At the time, the United States was not involved in the war, and Kreisler was hailed by the public as a wounded war hero who had returned to the violin in spite of his injuries. The following year,

Fritz Kreisler performing a recital in London's Albert Hall in 1932. Although internationally famous, Kreisler's popularity with American audiences was tainted because he served in the Austrian army during World War I. *Reproduced by permission of AP/Wide World Photos, Inc.*

Kreisler's memoir titled, *Four Weeks in the Trenches: The War Story of a Violinist,* which told the story of his short-lived experiences on the Eastern Front, was published. In the book Kreisler explains that his musical background was of great help to him and his regiment because his highly trained ear enabled him to determine the exact locations from which the enemy's shells were being fired. Kreisler also wrote that "War may bring unspeakable horrors, but it does not fail to unfold the finest flowerings of humanity." He then explained: "I have seen acts of the most tender sympathy and kindness, and real heroism," adding that "In the mass we hated our enemy, but as soon as we were confronted with him in person, all was kindness to the individual. I have seen emaciated [thin and starving] Austrian soldiers . . . hand a crust of bread to a Russian prisoner." Kreisler expressed the hope that after the war, artists like himself would help carry the message of peace around the world: "Surely art and religion will be the first forces that will set about the great reconstruction of world sympathy."

When Austria's emperor Franz Josef died in November 1916, Kreisler wrote a tribute to him in the *New York Times Magazine.* This article and Kreisler's record of military service in 1914 were used as weapons against him in 1917 when the United States entered the war on the side of the Allies. On November 8, Kreisler was forbidden to perform in a concert in Pittsburgh after protests by patriotic organizations persuaded local officials to declare that the violinist's appearance there would be a threat to public safety. Kreisler was escorted by the local police onto a train for New York. Officials in several other U.S. cities also banned Kreisler's appearances, and he was forced to abandon his concert tour. During the Pittsburgh controversy, he issued a statement freely acknowledging his service in the Austrian army but declared that he had made monetary gifts to Austrian friends and charities purely out of humanitarian motives. Kreisler's statement continued: "During every minute of my three years' stay in this country I have been conscious of my duty to it in return for the hospitality. I have obeyed its laws in letter and spirit and I have not done anything that might be construed in the least as being detrimental to it. Not a penny of my earnings has ever nor will it ever, contribute to the purchase of rifles and ammunition, no matter where and in whatsoever cause."

Postwar Redemption

After World War I ended in 1918, Kreisler waited a year before resuming his public appearances in the United States. On October 7, 1919, his operetta *Apple Blossoms* opened to critical acclaim in New York City. Three weeks later he appeared at New York's Carnegie Hall in a benefit performance for the Vienna Children's Milk Relief. He was met with resounding ovations, though the American Legion tried to prevent his appearances in other American cities, or at least to prevent him from playing music by German composers. Gradually, the wartime animosities were forgotten, and Kreisler reclaimed his status as a beloved violinist. In 1921, he turned down an offer to become conductor of the St. Louis Symphony. That year, in his essay "Music and Life," Kreisler wrote glowingly of music as a unifying force: "Music belongs to no nation. The spell of music is the same [in all countries]. Music, like art and literature, is universal, it transcends all national boundaries." In

The Red Scare and Fears of Leftist Radicalism

When World War I ended, America shifted from anti-German sentiment to public fear of a new enemy—radical leftist politics. The rise of leftist organizations was symbolized by the new government in Russia: Led by Vladimir Lenin, the Bolsheviks—or Reds—a revolutionary group, had toppled the Russian czar in 1917. The Reds believed that common people—not the czar or other conservative leaders—should have power. Labor and racial unrest in the United States, combined with the growing membership of the Communist Party, worried some American government officials and led them to warn against a leftist takeover—the "Red menace." The most prominent of these voices was A. Mitchell Palmer, President Woodrow Wilson's new attorney general. Palmer asked Special Assistant J. Edgar Hoover to organize a new intelligence division for the Justice Department to investigate radical activities in the United States. This new division was the forerunner of the Federal Bureau of Investigation (FBI).

During 1919, fear turned to panic. In many cities across the country, police raided the offices of radical groups that they considered to be anti-government. In May, a mob in New York City attacked the editorial offices of the socialist newspaper, *The New York Call*. In November, federal agents arrested two hundred members of the Union of Russian Workers at the newspaper's headquarters on charges of sending traitorous materials through the mail. The U.S. House of Representatives refused to seat a socialist member, Victor Berger of Wisconsin, and the New York state legislature expelled five members who had been elected on the socialist ticket.

The Red Scare reached its peak with the so-called Palmer Raids of January 2, 1920, when Palmer ordered the arrest of ten thousand people in thirty-three cities for alleged subversive activities. Palmer's order violated constitutional protections against unreasonable search and seizure. Many people were sent to jail without hearings, and six hundred foreigners were deported (returned to their countries of citizenship). Even though the panic subsided soon after the Palmer Raids, the Red Scare had a chilling effect on people who held political beliefs that were outside the mainstream. In the end, the Red Scare dealt a crippling blow to socialist and other left-wing movements in the United States.

1923, after a successful concert tour of Japan, Korea, and China, Kreisler and his wife settled into their first permanent home, in Berlin. (This home was later destroyed in an Allied air raid during World War II.)

During the next fifteen years, Kreisler performed in hundreds of concerts all over the world. In 1932, his second comic opera, *Sissy,* premiered in Vienna. When the Nazis, a German political movement led by Adolf Hitler that promoted racism and the expansion of state power, annexed Austria in 1938, Kreisler was again drafted into military service; but he became a French citizen and, with his wife, escaped to the United States as a refugee just weeks after World War II began in September 1939. (Kreisler became a U.S. citizen in 1943.) In 1941, Kreisler was seriously injured when he was hit by an egg-delivery truck on a Manhattan street, but he recovered and continued to perform until his retirement in 1950. Kreisler and his wife were together for sixty years. Kreisler died on January 29, 1962. His wife, Harriet, survived him by only sixteen months.

With the advent of recording equipment, Kreisler was able to reach people like no other performing had done previously In summarizing Kreisler's career biographer Amy Biancolli writes, "Was Kreisler the most revered violinist of his generation? Yes. Of any generation? Possibly. By almost any reckoning, Kreisler's popularity was of a scope and depth that the world had not seen before and possibly will not again."

For More Information

Books

Biancolli, Amy. *Fritz Kreisler: Love's Sorrow, Love's Joy.* Portland, Ore.: Amadeus Press, 1998.

Kreisler, Fritz. *Four Weeks in the Trenches: The War Story of a Violinist.* New York: Houghton Mifflin, 1915. Reprint, Neptune City, NJ: Paganiniana Publications, 1981.

Lochner, Louis P. *Fritz Kreisler.* New York: Macmillan, 1950.

Web sites

"Four Weeks in the Trenches." [Online] http://www2.h~net.msu.edu/~habsweb/sourcetexts/kreis1.htm (accessed April 2001).

"Fritz Kreisler." [Online] http://www.geocities.com/Vienna/1066/kreisler.html (accessed April 2001).

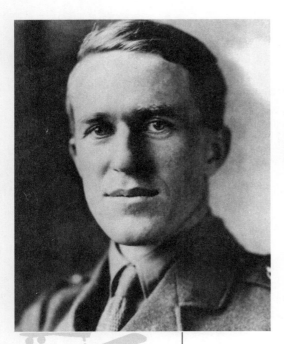

T. E. Lawrence

August 15, 1888
Tremadoc, North Wales
May 13, 1935
Bovington Camp, Dorset, England

Scholar, writer, soldier, and adventurer

> "I've been and am absurdly overestimated. There are no supermen and I'm quite ordinary, and will say so whatever the artistic results. In that point I'm one of the few people who tell the truth about myself."
>
> —*From T. E. Lawrence,* The Seven Pillars of Wisdom.

T. E. Lawrence. *Reproduced by permission of Archive Photos, Inc.*

Scholar, writer, soldier, and adventurer, Thomas Edward Lawrence became an unwilling figure of exotic romance and daring during World War I. A student and admirer of Arab culture, Lawrence devoted his young adulthood to trying to help the Arab people achieve independence. The failure to achieve this goal, however, left him broken and disappointed, and he spent the rest of his life trying to escape the fame and public adoration that he had never wanted. Though many people honored him as a glamorous hero, others thought he was a conceited fraud who did not deserve the place he was given in history, as Lawrence of Arabia.

A Young Knight Prepares for His Quest

All of his life T. E. Lawrence was an eccentric, a misfit who never did things in the ordinary way. Even in his early childhood, he stood out from other children as a serious boy, obsessed with history by the age of eight. He was particularly fond of studying the Middle Ages (A.D. 500–500), and he tried to imitate the behavior of the knights of that period, who lived by the code of honor and chivalry (the practices of knighthood).

As a boy, Lawrence was horrified to discover that he and his four brothers were illegitimate (born out of wedlock). His father, who went by the name of Robert Lawrence, was really an Anglo-Irish nobleman named Sir Robert Chapman. Years before young Thomas's birth, Chapman had abandoned his family and position to run away with his daughters' nanny, Sarah. Together they set up a new household in Wales, pretending to be married, and took the last name of Lawrence. Throughout his life, Lawrence would feel ashamed that his parents had not been married.

A small man (5 feet 5 inches at adulthood) who always wished he was bigger, Lawrence enjoyed testing his physical limits. As a child, he invented physical tests for himself, the way he imagined the knights of the Middle Ages might have. When he was a teenager, he took a long bicycling trip through France. In 1907, he got a scholarship to Jesus College at Oxford University and began his study of history in earnest. Still fascinated by the Middle Ages, he decided in the summer of 1909 to make a walking tour of Syria and study the castles left there by the crusaders. (The crusaders were Christian knights who traveled from Europe to the Middle East between the eleventh and thirteenth centuries to try to recapture the Holy Land from the Islamic people who had conquered the area.) During that hot summer, Lawrence walked more than a thousand miles. Although he was robbed and beaten along the way, he was accepted into Arab villages with warm hospitality. He visited many medieval castles and made notes and sketches, which he used in the paper he wrote when he returned to Oxford. He received praise and excellent marks on his paper, but his trip had given him much more: a love of Arab lands and a desire to learn more about them.

The Scholar Becomes a Soldier

In 1911, Lawrence returned to the Middle East, this time with a British Museum archeological team, to excavate an ancient site at Carchemish in Syria. He worked there until 1914, learning the Arabic language and exploring the region as far as the Sinai peninsula. When World War I broke out in 1914, Lawrence joined the British army and was sent to Cairo, Egypt, to work in intelligence (gaining information about the enemy). His knowledge of the region made him helpful in the

Although he was British, T. E. Lawrence developed a great love for Arab culture and fought passionately for Arab independence. *Photograph courtesy of The Library of Congress.*

map department, and his fluency in Arabic and respect for the Arab people made him valuable as a messenger between the Arabs and the British.

In 1916, Lawrence was sent on a mission to ask for support from a local Arab leader. At that time, the entire Middle East was under the control of the Ottoman Empire, which had joined Germany in its fight against the British and their allies in World War I. The British hoped to encourage the Arabs to rebel against the Ottoman Turks. If the Arabs could defeat the Ottoman Turks, the British promised, the Arab states would be rewarded with gold and weapons and independence when the war was over. Lawrence not only took this message to the Arab leader Husayn ibn 'Alî, but he stayed with Hussein to help the Arabs in their revolt against the Turks. Along with Hussein's son, Faisal, Lawrence led the ragged Arab troops against huge Turkish armies.

Though he had not been a soldier long and had never studied military strategy, Lawrence had experience supervising Arab workers on the archeological site, and he put that experience to good use. He was able to help unite the many Arab tribes into a single force, and together they struck at the Turks all over the Hejaz area, in what is now Saudi Arabia. Lawrence used daring guerrilla tactics with brave bluffs and many small, sudden attacks to stun the Turkish forces in battles like Wadi Run, in what is now Jordan. Lawrence's Arab armies cut off the Hejaz railroad and overran Damascus in Syria. By 1917, the British, under General Edmund Allenby, were able to invade and take the Arab countries from the Turks.

Betrayal and Disillusionment

It soon became apparent that British promises of Arab independence had been outright lies. At the same time the British had gained Arab support with promises of independence, they also had privately promised Palestinian Jews a homeland in Palestine, a country that most Arabs considered Arabic. But before the British had made promises to either the Arabs or the Palestinian Jews, they had secretly signed the SykesPicot Agreement with France. In this official document, France and England agreed to divide much of the Ottoman Empire between them, with France taking Syria and Lebanon, and Britain taking Palestine and Iraq.

When he found out about SykesPicot, Lawrence felt shocked, angry, and personally betrayed. Worse, he felt that he had betrayed the trust of Faisal and the other Arabs who had become his friends and comrades. However, he still believed that he could change the minds of those in power. When the war ended, he went to the Paris Peace Conference to plead for Arab independence. Dressed in the long robes he had worn when he lived among the Arabs, Lawrence was an impressive

Lawrence the Writer

A lifelong scholar, Lawrence was a productive writer, keeping detailed journals and writing long letters to friends and family throughout his life. In 1919, while still at the Paris Peace Conference, he began to compile the extensive notes he had written during the two years he had been on the march with the Arab armies. Working from these notes, his accounts to his British superiors in Cairo, and his memories, he started to write a long account of his years in the Middle East. Unfortunately, the manuscript was lost, and Lawrence had already destroyed the notes he used to write it, so he was forced, late in 1919, to begin the painful process of recreating his work.

The Seven Pillars of Wisdom was finally published privately in 1926 (which meant that Lawrence arranged to have a publisher to print a small number of books that were not sold in bookstores). Lawrence did not want the book to be commercially published and sold in bookstores, and it was not—until after his death in 1935. A shorter version of his story, called *Revolt in the Desert,* was published in 1927. It sold enough copies to pay off all of Lawrence's debts. *The Mint,* a much praised account of Lawrence's years in the air force and Royal Tank Corps, was written under the pen name John Ross. This work was tucked away with Lawrence's papers and not published until 1955.

In 1935, to earn money during his retirement, Lawrence published a translation of the Greek epic poem the *Odyssey.* Written around 700 B.C. by Homer, the *Odyssey* is the story of a soldier's long and difficult journey home, a story that Lawrence understood perhaps only too well.

figure as he passionately demanded justice for the Arab people. However, he failed to convince those who had much more to gain from European dominance of the region.

Lawrence returned home to face an image of himself that the media had created while he was at war. Journalists who had seen Lawrence in action fighting with the Arab troops had sent back reports of an impossibly romantic figure, a dashing English officer in flowing Arab robes, thundering across the desert. One American reporter, Lowell Thomas, wrote a book and developed a stage show about the feats of the soldier he called "Lawrence of Arabia." Audiences in England and the United States were entranced by this romanticized picture of a bold and exotic war hero.

Far from being a hardened war hero, Lawrence was devastated by his wartime experiences and bitter that he could not keep his promise of freedom to the Arab people. War had not been an exotic adventure, but a series of extreme hardships. He had been sick with dysentery, malaria, and deep, festering saddle sores. He had been captured by Turks in the town of Deraa, tortured, and perhaps raped. He was so angry about the British involvement in SykesPicot that he refused the medals and honors he was offered for his military service.

Demonstrating what some would call his emotional instability and others would call extreme shyness, Lawrence abandoned his famous identity in 1922 and enlisted in the Royal Air Force (RAF) under the name John Ross. Within a year, the press had discovered him, and he was forced to leave the air force. But he did not give up his efforts to disappear. Using the name T. E. Shaw, he enlisted in the Royal Tank Corps, remaining there for several years, then transferring to the RAF. He served in the air force as Thomas Shaw until he reached the military retirement age of forty-six. He retired reluctantly to a tiny cottage in Dorset, England, where he lived until his death in a motorcycle accident in 1935. The eccentric misfit who had wanted only to be left alone was now the property of the public: Since the biography by his friend Robert Graves, published in 1927, there have been more than fifty biographies of T. E. Lawrence as well as an epic film—Lawrence of Arabia—made by David Lean in 1962, all trying to capture the many sides of this complex man.

For More Information

Books

Brown, Malcolm. *A Touch of Genius: The Life of T. E. Lawrence.* New York: Paragon House, 1989.

Knightley, Phillip. *Lawrence of Arabia.* Nashville, TN: T. Nelson, 1977.

Articles

Belt, Don, and Annie Griffiths Belt. "Lawrence of Arabia: A Hero's Journey." *National Geographic,* January 1999, 38–41.

Reid, Holden Brian. "Lawrence and the Arab Revolt." *History Today,* May 1985, 41–45.

Waters, Irene. "The Lawrence Trail." *Contemporary Review* 272, no. 1587 (1998): 205–11.

Vladimir Lenin

April 22, 1870
Simbirsk, Russia
January 21, 1924
Gorki, Russia

Political leader, revolutionary

Vladimir Lenin.

Vladimir Lenin was one of the most influential political leaders of the twentieth century. Born into a Russia that still had one foot in the Middle Ages (A.D. 500–c. 1500), he led a political movement that became the revolution that created the Soviet Union. Though many people criticize Lenin as a dictator and a terrorist, it must be acknowledged that he developed the practical theory of modern communism, organized the defeat of one of the most brutal monarchies in the world, and began the process that would make the Soviet Union a modern nation. Lenin dreamed of a world where working people would control their own governments. Though his dream has not been realized yet, his work and ideas did lead to a consciousness of the working class that has resulted in improved conditions for working people worldwide.

A Radical Emerges from the Nobility

Vladimir Lenin was born Vladimir Ilich Ulyanov on April 22, 1870, in Simbirsk, a small town in the western part of Russia. He was the third of seven children, though two of his siblings died as babies. Lenin's ancestors were serfs (servants who were bound to the land they worked), but by the time of Lenin's birth, his family had begun to climb the social ladder. His father, Ilya, became a teacher and worked his way up to the position of inspector of schools. A dedicated and principled man, Ilya Ulyanov later achieved the position of director of schools, which brought with it the status of nobility. Because of this, Lenin was born with noble rank and had a fairly sheltered childhood. His mother, Maria, taught him the love of literature and music. From her he learned to play the piano, and for the rest of his life he would turn to music when he felt torn and stressed from his political work.

Lenin was a wild and rowdy child, with a tendency toward meanness and tantrums. He was an excellent student, but he could be conceited and harsh toward his fellow students. He loved his family deeply, especially his older brother, Alexander, a student and political activist in St. Petersburg. When Lenin Vladimir was a teenager, two events occurred that ended his peaceful childhood forever: In 1886, his father died suddenly of a stroke. A year later Alexander, who had been plotting with a group of revolutionaries to assassinate Czar Alexander III (the emperor of Russia), was caught by the police and hanged.

His brother's death affected Lenin deeply. He was suddenly the man of the family at age sixteen; he had lost his father and his adored brother; and because his brother had been executed as a traitor, Lenin Vladimir was mocked and insulted by those who assumed he must be a revolutionary too. The headmaster of his school stood by him and recommended him for acceptance into law school at Kazan University, but Lenin's university career would not last long. He joined a group of students who were protesting the closure of school fraternities and was expelled, mostly because of his brother's previous political activities. Angered at being expelled when he had done nothing wrong, and with no schoolwork to occupy him, Lenin turned to revolutionary politics himself. He began to read *Das Kapital* by Karl Marx (1818–1883), a book that described a radical new system of government that would divide resources more equally among members of society—this new system was called communism.

Exile and Activism

After being expelled from the University of Kazan because of his participation in a political rebellion, Lenin continued to study on his own and earned his law degree in 1891. While practicing law in the town of Samara, near where he had grown up, he met other anticzarist revolutionaries, among whom he continued to develop his political ideas. When a famine struck Samara in 1891 and 1892, Lenin began to display some of the political harshness that would mark his later career. He refused to help those who were suffering from the famine, because he felt that the terrible conditions of the people's lives would speed the revolution; helping people survive the famine would only postpone the needed changes.

By 1893, Lenin had moved to St. Petersburg, where he continued to study and began to write and distribute political pamphlets about socialism (a political and economic theory based on the idea of cooperation and shared resources for the common good), trying to stir up rebellion among the working people. He joined other agitators to form the League of Struggle for the Emancipation of the Working Class and was soon arrested for his political activities. From prison in St. Petersburg, he was sent to Siberia from 1897 to 1900. While in Siberia, Lenin met Nadezhda Krupskaya, another child of the nobility who had turned to radical politics. They married on July 22, 1898.

It was around this time that Vladimir Ilich Ulyanov began to write under the name Lenin to disguise his identity from authorities. Once his exile ended, Lenin started a radical newspaper called *Iskra* ("spark" in Russian). So that he could study, write, and publish *Iskra* more freely, he left Russia and went to Western Europe, traveling in Germany, England, and France and living in Switzerland, where he met exiled Russian Marxist Georgy Plekhanov. There Lenin wrote *What Is to Be Done?* (1902), an important work in which Lenin explained his theory that the workers could not create a revolution by themselves, but needed a strong intellectual political party to plan the overthrow of the czar and design the new government. In 1903, Lenin argued with the leadership of the Russian Social Democratic Workers' Party. The moderates, led by L. Martov (whose real name was Yuly Tsederbaum), wanted to keep the party open to all who agreed with its politics. The radicals, led by Lenin, insisted that only those truly committed to immediate revolution should be members. The party split between the radical Bolsheviks and the moderate Mensheviks.

War and Revolution

It was World War I that speeded revolution in Russia. Lenin was still in Western Europe when the war began in 1914, and he saw the war as an opportunity to advance the international workers' revolution he had worked for. He wrote and spoke, encouraging workers and soldiers of all countries to refuse to participate in the war. Meanwhile, in Russia, the war was taking not only most of the country's money, but also most of her men. With half of the workingmen in the army and no bread to feed those at home, the Russian people were desperate. Czar Nicholas II (1868–1918), a weak and confused ruler under the influence of his wife Alexandra (1872–1918) and her corrupt advisor Rasputin (1872?–1916), could not deal with Russia's problems. On March 8, 1917, a march to demand food turned into a riot with workers and peasants storming the czar's palace.

In Switzerland, Lenin read the news of the overthrow of the czar. German authorities, anxious to do anything that might destabilize Russia and take her out of the war, helped Lenin return to his country. There he led the Bolsheviks in the overthrow of the provisional (temporary) government. In November 1917, Lenin was named chief commissar (a Communist party official) of Russia. By March 1918, as Russia plunged deeper into civil war, Lenin ordered his negotiator and fellow revolutionary Leon Trotsky (1879–1940) to sign an armistice (peace treaty) with Germany, ending Russia's involvement in World War I.

Though the international revolution Lenin had hoped for did not happen, the Russian Revolution was under way, and it was bloody. The White Army, or the soldiers of the old nobility, fought against the Bolsheviks (also called Reds) for control of the country. Although Lenin called for elections for a national assembly, he almost immediately dissolved the elected body and made himself dictator. Lenin felt that he needed to be ruthless and severe to establish his new form of socialism. He established the Cheka, a secret police that arrested or killed those who opposed the new government. By

Vladimir Lenin addressing a crowd in Moscow, Russia, after he was named chief commissar in 1917.
Reproduced by permission of Archive Photos, Inc.

1921, the Bolsheviks had won the civil war, and Lenin was the established leader of the new Russia. He had survived an assassination attempt in August 1918, and many of his enemies were dead, in prison, or in concentration camps.

Though Lenin continued to work long, stressful hours setting up new political and economic policies in Russia, the endless work of the revolution had taken its toll on his health.

He had a stroke on May 26, 1922, and it permanently weakened him. After two more debilitating strokes, he died of a fourth stroke on January 21, 1924.

After Lenin's death, his wife, Nadezhda Krupskaya, pleaded with the Russian people, "Do not let your sorrow be transformed into demonstrations of adoration of Vladimir Ilich's personality. Do not put up buildings or monuments in his name. When he was alive he set little store by such things; indeed, he actively disliked them," as quoted in a *Time* magazine article, "But Can They Repair a Broken Reputation?" Nonetheless, the Russian people were not ready to lose their dynamic leader so soon after the revolution. The name of Lenin's birthplace, Simbirsk, was changed to Ulyanovsk to honor him, and the name of the ancient city of St. Petersburg was changed to Leningrad. Lenin's body was embalmed and put on display in a large mausoleum in Moscow's Red Square, where it gained the status of a national monument. Through the decades, thousands of Russians and foreign tourists have filed by to pay their respects to Lenin's remains.

With the fall of the Soviet Union and its Communist government in 1991, Lenin's reputation as a heroic leader has suffered. The name Leningrad was dropped in favor of the city's former name, St. Petersburg. The statue of Lenin in Red Square was pulled down, and new Russian leaders debate removing his mausoleum as well. Some even suggested burying Lenin next to the recently discovered remains of Czar Nicholas II to symbolize a healing of old conflicts. While they debate about what to do, Lenin's body remains in Red Square, but he has competition he might never have expected: In 1990, the Moscow McDonald's surpassed Lenin's tomb as the most-visited spot in Red Square.

For More Information

Books

Haney, John. *Vladimir Ilich Lenin*. New York: Chelsea House, 1988.

Liversidge, Douglas. *Lenin: Genius of Revolution*. New York: Franklin Watts, 1969.

Resnick, Abraham. *Lenin: Founder of the Soviet Union*. Chicago: Children's Press, 1987.

Volkogonov, Dmitri. *Lenin: A New Biography*. New York: The Free Press, 1994.

Articles

"But Can They Repair a Broken Reputation?" *Time,* 1 February 1999, 18.

Friedrich, Otto. "Headed for the Dustheap: How Lenin's Party Rose to Power and Then Disintegrated Is This Century's Most Gripping Tale." *Time,* 19 February 1990, 36–39.

Web sites

The Lenin House. [Online] http://www.geocities.com/CapitolHill/Senate/6174 (accessed March 2001).

Lenin Internet Archive. [Online] http://www.marxists.org/archive/lenin/ (accessed March 2001).

Vladimir Ilich Lenin Home Page. [Online] http://www.soften.ktu.lt/~kaleck/Lenin (accessed March 2001).

Vladimir Lenin. [Online] http://www.acerj.com/CommOnline/Leninbio.htm (accessed March 2001).

Erich Ludendorff

April 9, 1865
Kruszewnia, Prussia
December 20, 1937
Munich, Germany

German general

By August 1916 the German army was struggling to survive a war it thought it should be winning. The great assault on the French fortresses at Verdun—which German general Erich von Falkenhayn (1861–1922) thought would "bleed France white" and crush the Allies' will to fight—had turned into a six-month-long bloodbath. German military and political leaders pushed Kaiser Wilhelm II (1859–1941), the German emperor, for a change. Late in August, the kaiser called on the country's two most illustrious military leaders: General Paul von Hindenburg (1847–1934) and his second in command, General Erich Ludendorff. Hindenburg and Ludendorff had become heroes by beating the Russians on the Eastern Front; now they would be given unprecedented powers to direct the German war effort on the crucial Western Front. For the next two years, Hindenburg and Ludendorff squeezed every last drop of effort from the German army and the German people in the attempt to conquer the Allies.

Destined to Be a Soldier

Erich Ludendorff was born to be a soldier: Both his father and maternal grandfather had been officers in the Pruss-

"Every human life is war in miniature. In internal affairs, the political parties fight for power just as in diplomacy the great powers do so. This will always be the case because it is the law of nature.... Human nature is war."

—*From Erich Ludendorff, Kriegfuhrung und Politik.*

Erich Ludendorff. *Reproduced by permission of Hulton-Deutsch Collection/Corbis-Bettmann.*

ian cavalry. But Erich Ludendorff was not born to be a general. In Prussia (the dominant state in the cluster of Germanic states that would unify into the nation of Germany in 1871) generals came from the nobility. A person of noble birth was marked by the designation "von" before his last name. Ludendorff, born on April 9, 1865, was a commoner, raised in a struggling family that lived in the province of Posen. To reach the top of the German armed forces, he would have to work unrelentingly—and that is what he did.

At the age of twelve Ludendorff entered cadet school at Holstein. Ludendorff was mocked by his fellow cadets because his last name lacked the "von" of nobility, and he was driven to his physical limit by the demanding Prussian officers who ruled the school. Perhaps because of these difficulties, Ludendorff became ever more focused and severe, devoting all his waking hours to making himself the best possible soldier. After graduating from the Lichterfelde Military Academy in Berlin at the top of his class, Ludendorff won a commission as a lieutenant in 1882. Just twelve years later, after passing every test that was placed before him, Ludendorff was appointed to the prestigious German general staff, the group of officers who prepared war plans and strategy for the commanding general of the army. At the age of twenty-nine, Ludendorff had become one of Germany's premier soldiers.

"A Man of Iron Principles"

For the next twenty years, Ludendorff devoted himself to understanding every area of the German military. In 1908 he was appointed to lead the mobilization and deployment (gathering and transport of military supplies) division of the general staff, a position for which he had been trained by Field Marshal Count Alfred von Schlieffen (1833–1913), the mastermind of German war plans. Ludendorff longed for the day when his years of study and preparation would place him in the position of leadership that he felt he so richly deserved.

Ludendorff's years of devotion to the military had made him an unpleasant man. German officers were known for their arrogance and their rudeness to their subordinates, but Ludendorff was more rude and arrogant than most. Robert B. Asprey, author of *The German High Command at War*, describes Ludendorff as "generally tense, cold as a fish, a monocled [an eyeglass for one eye] humorless eye staring from a heavily jowled red face as he barked orders in a high, nasal voice, his second (and later third) chin quivering from the effort. He was rigid and inflexible in thought, given to sudden rages, a table banger, frequently rude to subordinates, often tactless to superiors." According to Red Reeder, author of *Bold Leaders of World War I,* Ludendorff's medical director said that the general's devotion to work was so intense that "He has never seen a flower bloom or heard a bird sing." According to Asprey, Ludendorff's wife described her husband as "a man of iron principles."

Trial by Fire

Ludendorff greeted the coming of World War I in August 1914 with excitement and anticipation: He had been training for this moment all his life. Joining in the German effort to cross Belgium and storm into France, Ludendorff was made first quartermaster general. He was in charge of providing food, clothing, transportation, and supplies to the troops attacking the Belgian fortress city of Liège. Observing the battle from behind the lines, Ludendorff grew impatient when the superior German army could not break through the well-fortified Belgian lines. When a battlefield general was killed in action, Ludendorff moved to the front lines to take his place. Seizing a captured Belgian car, Ludendorff drove toward a small tower that the Germans had been trying to capture. According to Reeder, "Ludendorff jumped out. He drew his sword as if he were attacking the fort singlehanded. He pounded on the gate with the hilt of his weapon and shouted, 'Surrender! In the name of Kaiser Wilhelm.'"

Ludendorff's bold action energized the German troops, who soon overwhelmed the outnumbered Belgians. It also earned Ludendorff the nickname of "Hero of Liège" and a prestigious military medal, the *Ordre pour le Mérite,* from Kaiser Wilhelm II. Perhaps most important, Ludendorff's leadership at Liège convinced Chief of the General Staff Helmuth Johannes von Moltke (1848–1916) that Ludendorff's skills were needed in a spot where German soldiers were not faring so well: the Eastern Front.

Paul von Hindenburg (left) and Erich Ludendorff discuss strategy for the German army during World War I. *Reproduced by permission of Corbis Corporation.*

Tannenberg and Beyond

In August 1914, the Russian army had surprised the Germans with an unexpectedly strong attack on Germany's easternmost province of Prussia, home of Kaiser Wilhelm II. Even worse, the German general in charge had panicked and ordered his army to retreat. Ludendorff seemed the perfect man to coordinate the troops and supplies that would be needed to stop the Russian advance. However, because he was not nobility, he could not command an army. So the German general staff tapped retired general Paul von Hindenburg to take the command, with Ludendorff as his chief of staff. Though the two men had never met, they soon learned to work together well: Ludendorff made all of the important plans and decisions, and Hindenburg gave the orders.

Within days of taking charge, Ludendorff had reorganized the German war effort and launched an attack on the Russians. Exploiting Russian mistakes and a deep hatred between two Russian generals, Ludendorff and Hindenburg's troops soon routed the Russians, taking ninety thousand Russian prisoners and causing another fifty thousand Russian casualties in the Battle of Tannenberg. This battle was one of the most decisive victories in a war that soon became known more for its stalemates than for its dramatic triumphs. But Ludendorff and Hindenburg did not stop there. For the next two years they drove Russian troops backward all across the Eastern Front, scoring a string of victories that stood in sharp contrast to the deadlock along the Western Front. By 1916 many within the German military believed that only Hindenburg and Ludendorff—widely known as "The Duo" or simply "HL"—could win the war on the Western Front.

Total War

When Ludendorff and Hindenburg were asked to lead the German war effort on the Western Front in August 1916, they were given unprecedented powers. Hindenburg was named chief of the general staff, and Ludendorff became his first quartermaster general—a title he preferred to "second general" because he did not want to be second at anything. The two believed that the only way to win was with the all out support of the entire German people and the fullest extension of German military efforts. With the kaiser's support, Ludendorff and Hindenburg schemed to remove any general or politician who opposed their plan for winning the war. By February 1917 they had removed the statesmen who opposed unrestricted submarine warfare. In that same month they sent out German submarines to try to disrupt English shipping so severely that England would be driven from the war. By July 1917 Ludendorff and Hindenburg told Kaiser Wilhelm II that he must get rid of the chancellor, Theobald von Bethmann Hollweg (1856–1921), who wished to negotiate for peace, or else they would resign. Bethmann Hollweg was forced out, and Ludendorff and Hindenburg assumed nearly complete control of the German government. From that point on, Germany was in essence a military dictatorship, with Ludendorff calling all the shots.

Ludendorff and Hindenburg were not directly involved in planning battles, and they rarely traveled to the front to see soldiers in action. Instead they stayed at their comfortable headquarters and made plans that they asked others to carry out. In 1917, as the Russian government collapsed, they helped political leader Vladimir Lenin (1870–1924) enter Russia so he could lead a socialist revolution there. This was a strategic move by Ludendorff and Hindenburg since they knew that the socialists would not support the war. After leading a successful overthrow of the Russian government, Lenin's negotiator, Leon Trotsky (1879–1940) signed a peace treaty with Germany in 1918 that removed Russia from the war. By eliminating the fight against Russia on the Eastern Front, Ludendorff and Hindenburg could turn their full attention to the fighting on the Western Front.

The Last Offensive

For spring 1918, Ludendorff and Hindenburg planned a huge German offensive that they hoped would finally force the Allies to retreat. Ludendorff wanted to strike quickly, before American forces could arrive to fortify the Allied troops. Beginning on March 21, 1918, the Germans launched their spring offensive with fierce attacks on the Somme River, the Belgian town of Ypres, and the Chemin des Dames. They had great success, pushing the Allies back more than forty miles in some places, but at a stunning cost—the Germans lost more than six hundred thousand men in less than three months of fighting. Even so, Ludendorff and Hindenburg ordered the onslaught to continue. Two more major assaults were launched in June and July, and both were disasters. The Allies stood firm and in some places pushed the Germans back. German soldiers, convinced that their leaders were sending them to slaughter, deserted in great numbers. By mid-July the German push had turned into a massive German retreat. On hearing of the setbacks, the German Chancellor, Georg von Hertling, wrote that "even the most optimistic among us knew that all was lost," as quoted in Martin Gilbert's *The First World War*.

Though they were far from the battlefields, Ludendorff and Hindenburg recognized that the end was near for the German war effort. According to James Stokesbury, author of *A Short History of World War I*, when Ludendorff learned of the German retreat in late July 1918, he went to see Hindenburg and asked him what Germany ought to do. "Do? Do!" Hindenburg bellowed. "Make peace, you idiot!" But it was not that easy. Ludendorff knew that Germany needed to enter peace negotiations in a position of power. To do so, they would have to hold their ground on the Western Front and convince the Allies that Germany was an equal in power and not a defeated nation. Ludendorff and Hindenburg tried to marshal the remaining German troops to keep the enemy from entering Germany.

Through the late summer and into the early fall, Ludendorff and Hindenburg engineered a slow retreat in which the German army contested every inch of ground that they gave away. But with American troops adding fresh strength to the Allied line, the German cause was hopeless. Ludendorff grew increasingly distraught. According to Asprey, Hindenburg's physician became "concerned with Ludendorff's erratic ways marked by vicious outbursts of temper, restless nights broken by angry telephone calls to individual commanding generals, on occasion too much drinking, and crying spells." By late September generals began to report that Germany was facing total defeat. When one such report came in, writes Asprey, "There is some evidence that Ludendorff suffered a genuine fit, foaming at the mouth and collapsing on his office floor."

Shameful End

Though Ludendorff desperately tried to find some grounds on which to negotiate peace, it soon became clear that the Allies would not bargain with the military dictators who had led the German war effort. On October 25, 1918, in a humiliating interview with Kaiser Wilhelm II, Ludendorff was forced to resign. On November 9, Hindenburg resigned and the kaiser abdicated (gave up his throne). A new chancellor (a high state official) was appointed to negotiate peace terms, and Germany signed an armistice (peace treaty) on November 11, 1918. Despite the best efforts of Ludendorff and Hindenburg, the Germans had lost.

Ludendorff was not well liked in immediate postwar Germany. Threatened by revolutionaries who blamed Germany's problems on the generals, he fled the country wearing a wig and colored glasses and settled in Sweden. While in Sweden Ludendorff wrote his memoirs, in which he offered what has become known as the "stab-in-the-back" thesis, an explanation for the German defeat that suggests that unpatriotic forces in Germany kept the great nation from winning the war. This theory made Ludendorff popular with the nationalists (supporters of state power) who were coming to power in Germany during the early 1920s. Ludendorff moved back to Germany and participated in two attempts to unseat elected officials; the second attempt, in 1923, was organized by a young political agitator named Adolf Hitler (1889–1945). Ludendorff soon joined Hitler's National Socialist (or Nazi) Party, got elected to parliament, and campaigned for president in 1925. He was easily defeated by his former comrade—the man he had accused of betraying him and the nation—Paul von Hindenburg.

Defeated in politics as he had been in war, Ludendorff adopted strange and extreme beliefs. He subscribed to the mystical teachings of his second wife, Motile von Kemnitz, and began publishing a series of essays arguing that Jews and Freemasons (members of a fraternal organization) were to blame for keeping Germany from its rightful role as a world leader. Eventually he became so extreme and erratic in his pronouncements that even Hitler withdrew his support. Ludendorff died quietly on December 20, 1937, unmourned by a country that had once hailed him as a military hero.

For More Information

Books

Asprey, Robert B. *The German High Command at War: Hindenburg and Ludendorff Conduct World War I.* New York: William Morrow, 1991.

Gilbert, Martin. *The First World War: A Complete History.* New York: Henry Holt, 1994.

Ludendorff, Erich. *Kriegfuhrung und Politik.* Berlin: E. S. Mittler and Sohn, 1922.

Parkinson, Roger. *Tormented Warrior: Ludendorff and the Supreme Command.* London: Hodder and Stoughton, 1978.

Reeder, Red. *Bold Leaders of World War I.* Boston: Little, Brown, 1974.

Stokesbury, James L. *A Short History of World War I.* New York: William Morrow, 1981.

Mata Hari

August 7, 1876
Leeuwarden, Netherlands
October 15, 1917
Paris, France

Exotic dancer and courtesan

Mata Hari has gone down in history as one of the most notorious and exotic spies involved in World War I. Yet there is some evidence that her celebrated conviction for spying for the German army may have been based on false evidence. In fact, Mata Hari may not have been a spy at all. Rather, it is possible that she was a victim of a frantically suspicious world at war; unable to see the danger around her, she may have trapped herself in an attempt to make quick money. The whole truth about Mata Hari may never be known, but she was a flamboyant woman with a flair for the dramatic, so perhaps she would be pleased to know that her legend and her mystery live on.

A Childhood in the Netherlands

Mata Hari's original name was Margaretha Geertruida Zelle. She was the only girl of four children. Born in the ancient town of Leeuwarden, in the northern part of the Netherlands, Margaretha had striking looks and a dramatic nature even as a child. The only one in her family with dark hair and dark eyes, she took to telling people that she was half

"I am a neutral, but my sympathies are for France. If that does not satisfy you, do as you will."

—*Mata Hari, quoted in Erika Ostrovsky,* Eye of Dawn: The Rise and Fall of Mata Hari.

Mata Hari. *Reproduced by permission of Archive Photos, Inc.*

Indian or Indonesian. Adam Zelle, Margaretha's father, was a hatmaker. The family was only middle class, but Zelle was a pompous man who liked to dress and act like a fine gentleman. Though the neighbors often laughed at her father's bright clothes and fancy airs, Margaretha adored him. She was his special favorite, and as his hat shop prospered, he showered his little girl with gifts and affection.

However, Margaretha's happy childhood was cut short. When she was only thirteen, her father's business failed. The public shame of having no money when they had always put on a show of wealth was bad enough; it was worse, however, when her father abandoned the family. Within a year, her mother died, physically and emotionally broken by their troubles. The children were scattered among relatives; Margaretha was sent to live with her godfather in the tiny town of Sneek, not far from Leeuwarden. From there she was sent to school in nearby Leyde to learn to be a teacher.

Loss of Innocence and Escape through the Personal Ads

Margaretha did not learn to be a teacher, however. She had not been in school long when the headmaster noticed that his new student was strikingly beautiful. Though Margaretha was only fifteen, the headmaster began to pay her special attention, looking at her and touching her in ways that were appropriate for a lover, not a teacher. After a while, the other teachers and students noticed how the headmaster pursued Margaretha, and she was sent away from the school to stay with another relative.

Margaretha began to long for a family of her own and started reading the marriage ads in the local newspaper. One day she ran across a promising advertisement that had been placed by a captain on leave from service in the Dutch army. She answered the ad, and soon the eighteen-year-old Margaretha met the thirty-eight-year-old Captain Campbell MacLeod. Four months later, on July 11, 1895, they were married and traveled to Java, which was part of the Dutch East Indies (Dutch-controlled islands in the Pacific and Indian Oceans). Though Margaretha had wanted to travel and have adventures, her marriage was not a happy one. By 1902, she

and MacLeod had separated bitterly. Of their four children, one had died of disease, and two had been poisoned by a servant; her husband, who had turned out to be a brutal man, took the only surviving child from her.

A photograph of Mata Hari's home in France.

The Birth of Mata Hari

Heartsick and penniless after her failed marriage, Margaretha was still resourceful and hopeful. She went to Paris to seek work as an artist's model. She was unsuccessful at that, but she found another career that suited her much better. While living in Java with her husband, Margaretha had learned some of the sensual, snake dances that were sacred to the native people there. It was there, too, that she had first been given the name Mata Hari, which is a Malay expression meaning "eye of dawn" or "morning sun." In glittering Paris at the turn of the century, she found new uses for what she had learned during her unhappy marriage. Taking advantage of her exotic good looks, in 1905 Margaretha Geertruida Zelle became known as Mata Hari, the famous dancer.

Mata Hari gained wide fame as a dancer, combining the movements she had seen in Java with moves that she simply made up. Though she pretended to be a priestess from India dancing sacred religious rituals, her dances were very sexual. As she danced, she removed her clothes, becoming one of the first striptease dancers. Audiences loved her. After wild success in France, she performed her "sacred temple dances" in glamorous theaters from Spain to Egypt and became one of the most famous celebrities of her day. Although dance critics called her a fraud, many people were captivated by Mata Hari's mystery and sexuality.

It was not easy for a woman to earn a living on her own, but along with dancing, Mata Hari always had lovers to support her. She became the mistress to many men of high position during her dancing career, and when one relationship broke up, she would search for another. As she grew older and her fame as a dancer began to fade, she depended more and more on her affairs with men. A woman who receives money for having sexual affairs with wealthy men is called a courtesan, which is really the same as a prostitute.

Surviving in a World at War

When World War I broke out in August 1914, Mata Hari's constant travels around Europe, and her affairs with men on both sides of the war, brought her to the attention of the Allied authorities. They became convinced that she was a German spy. A French officer, Georges Ladoux, decided to try to get Mata Hari to become a double agent; in other words, he wanted her to pretend to continue to work for the Germans while actually spying for the Allies. There is little evidence that Mata Hari ever worked as a spy for the Germans, but she did accept Ladoux's proposal, agreeing to spy on the Germans for the French in exchange for good pay. There is also little evidence that she had strong political loyalty to either side. In fact, Mata Hari was a woman who had learned to do what she had to do to survive.

Though it is hard to know exactly what happened, it seems likely that Mata Hari did offer to spy for the Germans so

The Legend Lives On

The records of Mata Hari's trial were sealed by the French government for one hundred years, so the whole truth of her guilt or innocence will remain a mystery at least until the year 2017. However, the image of the glamorous, exotic spy captured the public imagination, and the name Mata Hari has remained famous for decades. Filmmakers began making movies of her life only two years after her death, and since then, artists in Germany, France, Spain, Italy, the United States, and other countries have created dozens of films, novels, and plays based on the dramatic life of Mata Hari. She has been portrayed by well-known actresses from many different countries, including Greta Garbo, Marlene Dietrich, and Jeanne Moreau. Even a cartoon show and an Internet search engine have been named for the famous spy.

Most of these fictional works take great liberties with the real life of Margaretha Geertruida Zelle, and most do not question whether she was, indeed, an effective spy for the Germans. However, many historians do question Mata Hari's guilt, and they have worked to clear her name. Her hometown in the Netherlands also hopes to prove Mata Hari's innocence. On the hundredth anniversary of her birth, the city of Leeuwarden opened a museum dedicated to Mata Hari and placed a statue of her nearby.

that she could spy on them for the French. The German officers she was involved with seemed to consider her something of a joke, though they did pay her for sex and gave her some unimportant information to pass along. They even gave her a code name—H21. The money and code name would be used against her during her trial for spying. It was the Germans who actually caused Mata Hari's arrest, by sending a message about her using her code name. Some historians suspect that the Germans did this on purpose, sending a message about Mata Hari in a code they knew the British had broken in order to distract the Allies from finding real German spies.

The French were fighting a hard and bloody war, however, and they took the German message very seriously. On February 13, 1917, Mata Hari was arrested by the French and spent five months in a grim prison in Paris. Her trial for espionage (spying) on July 24 and 25 was short and merciless. Mata Hari was accused of causing the deaths of more than fifty thousand Allied soldiers by passing vital secrets to the Germans. She was convicted unanimously and sentenced to death. She spent almost three more months in prison before she was taken out of her cell and shot by a firing squad. It is said that she smiled and blew a kiss to the men in the firing squad just before her death. Shortly after Mata Hari's execution, Ladoux, who had been largely responsible for her arrest and conviction, was arrested himself and imprisoned for espionage.

For More Information

Books

Howe, Russell Warren. *Mata Hari, The True Story.* New York: Dodd, Mead, 1986.

Keay, Julia. *The Spy Who Never Was: The Life and Loves of Mata Hari.* Santa Barbara, California, and Oxford, England: Clio Press, 1989.

Ostrovsky, Erika. *Eye of Dawn: The Rise and Fall of Mata Hari.* New York: Macmillan, 1978.

Articles

Howe, Russell Warren. "The Mournful Fate of Mata Hari, the Spy Who Wasn't Guilty." *Smithsonian,* May 1986, 132–49.

Films

Mata Hari: Seductive Spy. New York: Greystone Communications, for A&E Network, 1996.

Web sites

"Mata Hari." *The History of Espionage.* [Online] http://members.nbci.com/1spy/Mata_Hari.html (accessed February 2001).

"Mata Hari: Double Agent? One Truth." *Radio Netherlands Wereldomroep.* [Online] http://www.rnw.nl/holland/html/matahari_eng990228.html (accessed February 2001).

Wilfred Owen

**March 18, 1893
Oswestry, Shropshire, England
November 4, 1918
Sambre Canal, France**

Soldier and poet

S ome of the most powerful descriptions of war were written during World War I by the so-called war poets, mostly British soldiers in their twenties who wrote while fighting in France. Wilfred Owen is one of the most important war poets. He wrote eloquently about his service as an officer during the Battle of the Somme, which forced him to wrestle with the conflicts he saw between his duty as a soldier and his deep religious and pacifist beliefs. (Pacifists object to war as a means of settling disputes.) Owen strongly criticized the tragedy of war in his writings, but he fulfilled his military duty out of loyalty to his fellow soldiers. Helping lead his men across a canal in northern France exactly a week before the end of World War I, Owen was killed.

Budding Poet

Wilfred Edward Salter Owen was born in Oswestry, Shropshire, England, on March 18, 1893. He was the oldest of the four children born to Thomas Owen, a railroad station-master, and Susan Shaw Owen, the daughter of a prosperous family. Owen and his parents lived with his maternal grandfather until Wilfred was four; then his family moved to Birken-

"It is now possible to see that his gifts were not only gifts of genius, but other gifts that only the gods bestow. . . . He wrote more eloquently than other poets of the tragedy of boys killed in battle, because he felt that tragedy more acutely."

—*From Jon Stallworthy,* Wilfred Owen: A Biography.

Wilfred Owen. *Reproduced by permission of The Granger Collection, Ltd.*

111

The Poets of World War I

Since ancient times, poets of every culture have made war and soldiering important subjects of their work, in epic poems (long poems) that celebrate heroic exploits, in lyrics and odes that honor the courage of the warrior, or in pacifist works that criticize the brutality and horror of war. Some of the finest verses in the history of English literature were written by poets who served in World War I, many of whom died in combat while still in their twenties.

The following men are among the most prominent of the British war poets:

Rupert Brooke (1887–1915): After brief noncombat duty in Belgium, he died of an infection caused by a mosquito bite; he was serving in the Greek islands at the time. A sequence of sonnets (poems with fourteen lines and a definite rhyme pattern) titled *1914* contains his most famous lines: "If I should die, think only this of me: / That there's some corner of a foreign field / That is for ever England. . . ." Biographer Paul Delany calls Brooke "the most famous British hero of the war."

Robert Graves (1895–1985): Though he was severely wounded in combat in 1916, Graves lived to be ninety. He served as a captain with the Royal Welch Fusiliers during World War I and befriended another member of the regiment, poet Siegfried Sassoon. Graves's collection of war poems, *Fairies and Fusiliers,* helped establish his reputation as a literary figure after the war. The novel *I, Claudius* (1934) and the mythological study *The White Goddess* (1948) are his bestknown works. One of his sons was killed in World War II.

Isaac Rosenberg (1890–1918): The son of Russian Lithuanian immigrants to England, Rosenberg enlisted in the British army in 1915, and because he was rather short, he was assigned to the Bantam Battalion, a regiment made up of volunteers who were below the regulation minimum height of 5 feet 2 inches. In the

head, near Liverpool. Owen attended Birkenhead Institute until he was fourteen, when the family moved back to Shropshire, settling in the county seat at Shrewsbury. There, he attended Shrewsbury Technical School but failed in his efforts to win a scholarship to the University of London. He felt inclined toward religious work and accepted a position in which he received room and board in exchange for work with the vicar (a minister in charge of a church) of Dunsden in last two years of his brief life, Rosenberg wrote several important versedramas about Old Testament subjects, including *Moses* and *The Unicorn* (about King Saul and his wife). Two important poems that he wrote while in military service are titled "Marching" and "Break of Day in the Trenches." Critics regard Rosenberg's "Dead Man's Dump" (1917) as his finest "war" poem. Rosenberg was shot to death while on patrol duty during the Battle of the Somme on April 1, 1918.

Siegfried Sassoon (1886–1967): One of the poets who survived long after World War I, Sassoon befriended and encouraged such poets as Rupert Brooke, Robert Graves, and Wilfred Owen. Although he enlisted in the army and received awards for heroism, Sassoon became a pacifist and wrote an antiwar letter, "A Soldier's Declaration," that led some politicians to call for his courtmartial. With Robert Graves's help, Sassoon was committed to a mental hospital instead,

but he decided to return to combat so as not to betray his fellow soldiers. In 1919 *The War Poems of Siegfried Sassoon* was published. The final poem celebrates the armistice of 1918 in these words: ". . .O, but Everyone / Was a bird; and the song was wordless; the singing will never be done."

Edward Thomas (1878–1917): Killed on Easter Sunday, 1917, during the Battle of Arras, the thirty-nine-year-old Thomas was older than most of the other World War I poets, and he had already established his literary career before the war. He was strongly influenced by the American poet Robert Frost (1874–1963). "Rain," one of Thomas's most important "war" poems, written in 1916, includes these lines: "Rain, midnight rain, and nothing but wild rain / On this bleak hut, and solitude, and me / Remembering again that I shall die. . ." His wife, Helen Thomas, also was a noted poet.

Oxford. He left this position partly for health reasons and partly because he came to believe that the established church was failing in its duty to the poor. He returned to his family's home briefly, then accepted a position teaching at the Berlitz School of Languages in Bordeaux, France. During this period, Owen started writing poetry. He admired the writings of the Romantic poets, like John Keats, and he became friends with the poet Laurent Tailhade, who was a fellow pacifist.

A sign in wartime France warning that antigas precautions should be taken when passing beyond this point. Wilfred Owen's most famous poem, "Dulce et Decorum Est," was inspired by his disgust at the use of poisonous gas. *Reproduced by permission of Hulton Getty/Archive Photos, Inc.*

After World War I broke out, Owen returned to England and enlisted in the Artist's Rifles, a special air service regiment. Commissioned a lieutenant in 1916, he was sent to fight in France with the Lancashire Fusiliers. It was while he was serving that he began to write his finest poetry, which described in graphic detail the agonies of his fellow soldiers. His most famous poem, "Dulce et Decorum Est," was inspired by Owen's disgust at the use of mustard gas (a poisonous gas that has irritating effects to the body) against his fellow soldiers; the poem's ironic title is part of a Latin motto that means "Sweet and fitting it is to die for one's country." In Owen's judgment, no one who had experienced the horrors of battle would proclaim such patriotic sentiments. In this excerpt from the poem, Owen addresses those who believe in the glory and heroism of war: "If in some smothering dreams you too could pace / Behind the wagon that we flung him in / My friend, you would not tell with such high zest / To children ardent for some desperate glory, / The old lie: *Dulce et decorum est / Pro patria mori* [Sweet and fitting it is to die for one's country]."

Learning from Other Poets

As his time in the service dragged on, Owen became increasingly bitter about the harsh and brutal conditions of the battlefield. In letters to his mother and in poems, he expressed a deep pessimism about the war, and he began to criticize the political leaders who were, in his mind, responsible for the carnage (killing). In June 1917, suffering from shell shock (a nervous breakdown due to combat conditions), Owen was admitted to Craiglockhart War Hospital for Nervous Disorders near Edinburgh, Scotland. He became editor of the hospital's magazine, *The Hydra,* in which he published some of his poems as well as those of Siegfried Sassoon (1886–1967), another British soldier at the hospital, who went on to become a well-known poet. Owen also taught at a local school and played in an amateur orchestra. This helped him recover from his nervous disorder, and he began to write some of his best poetry.

Through Sassoon's influence, Owen met many of the other prominent poets of the time. Among the literary figures who became his friends and mentors were Robert Graves (1895–1985), Robert Ross (1869–1918), and Charles Scott-Moncrieff (1889–1930). Owen felt that his association with these men gave him the tools he needed to succeed as a poet. He wrote a letter to his mother, quoted in the *Norton Anthology of English Literature,* in which he compared himself to a ship able to sail on its own, without the assistance of tugboats: "I am a poet's poet. I am started. The tugs have left me. I feel a great swelling of the opening sea taking my galleon [large sailing ship]."

Return to the Battlefield

Despite his pacifist inclinations, Owen resolved to go back to the battlefield out of loyalty to his comrades and in order to write more authentically about the experiences of battle. On December 31, 1917, he wrote in his journal (quoted in the *Norton Anthology of English Literature*) about the terror he had once seen in his comrades' faces: "It will never be painted, and no actor will ever seize it. And to describe it, I think I must go back and be with them."

By August 1918, Owen had recovered from his illness well enough to return to France. He won a Military Cross for

Wilfred Owen's poems described the deplorable conditions that soldiers had to face on the battlefield, like this American soldier standing guard during a German gas attack in France. *Reproduced by permission of Hulton Getty/Archive Photos, Inc.*

bravery when he helped lead his company to safety during a battle. On November 4, while leading a group of soldiers across the Sambre Canal, Owen was killed in a hail of machinegun fire. He died four months short of his twenty-sixth birthday—and exactly one week before the armistice (peace treaty) of November 11 brought World War I to an end. . A few months before his death, Owen had written a preface for an edition of his poetry that he hoped to have published. In 1985, an excerpt from this preface—"My subject is War, and the pity of War. The poetry is in the pity. . ."—was carved into a monument that memorializes sixteen World War I poets in the Poets' Corner of Westminster Abbey in London.

Siegfried Sassoon knew the quality of Owen's verses and arranged to have twenty-three of Owen's poems published. The collection, titled *Poems,* appeared in 1920; it was edited by Edith Sitwell, a member of a prominent literary family in England. Her brother, Osbert Sitwell, had been a friend of Owen and Sassoon. In 1931, an expanded edition with twenty-nine poems was published, together with an introduction by Edmund Blunden, another notable British poet who had served in World War I. Owen's work has continued to inspire later generations of poets, such as Cecil DayLewis who in 1964 edited *The Collected Poems of Wilfred Owen,* which included seventy-nine poems.

For More Information

Books

Abrams, M.H., et al, editors. *Norton Anthology of English Literature.* Volume 2; 7th edition. New York: Norton, 2000.

Delany, Paul. *Rupert Brooke and the Ordeal of Youth.* New York: Free Press, 1987.

Owen, Wilfred. *Collected Letters.* London and New York: Oxford University Press, 1967.

Owen, Wilfred. *War Poems and Others.* London: Chatto and Windus, 1973.

Stallworthy, Jon. *Wilfred Owen: A Biography.* Oxford: Oxford University Press, 1975.

Sound Recordings

Britten, Benjamin. *War Requiem* (op. 66), 1962; recorded by Deutsche Grammophon, Hamburg, 1993.

Films

War Requiem. Directed by Derek Jerman. Mystic Fire Video, 1988. Videocassette.

Web sites

"The Poems of Wilfred Owen." [Online] http://www.pitt.edu/~novosel/owen.html (accessed April 2001).

"The War Poets Collection." [Online] http://www.napier.ac.uk/depts/library/craigcon/warpoets/warphome.htm (accessed April 2001).

"The Wilfred Owen Association." [Online] http://www.191418.co.uk/owen (accessed April 2001).

"WOMDA: The Wilfred Owen Multimedia Digital Archive." [Online] http://www.hcu.ox.ac.uk/jtap/ (accessed April 2001).

John Joseph Pershing

September 13, 1860
Laclede, Missouri
July 15, 1948
Washington, D.C.

Military leader

John Joseph Pershing.
Photograph courtesy of The Library of Congress.

General John Joseph Pershing is most famous for something he never said. The story goes that when he arrived in France in 1917, at the head of the American Expeditionary Forces (AEF), he dramatically declared, "Lafayette, we are here!" This was a reference to the Marquis de Lafayette (1757–1834), the French general who crossed the Atlantic during the American Revolution (1775–83) to fight alongside George Washington. More than a hundred years later, Pershing and the American forces were returning the favor—but it wasn't Pershing who made the stirring statement of this fact; it was one of his colonels, Charles Stanton. Indeed, such a statement would have been quite out of character for Pershing, who was noted for being a soldier and an administrator, but not one for having a way with words.

The Accidental Soldier

John Joseph Pershing was born on September 13, 1860, in Laclede, Missouri, on the eve of the Civil War. One of his earliest memories was of a band of Confederate soldiers raiding Laclede and creating terror. He had more positive memories of Union soldiers and even dressed up in a miniature Union army uniform, but he did not dream of a military career; instead, he began to think of becoming a lawyer. However, an economic depression in 1873 had caused problems for his formerly prosperous storekeeper father, and young Pershing had to find work. He taught school for a while, beginning in 1878. He studied for a teaching degree during vacation breaks and obtained the degree in 1880.

In 1881, Pershing applied to the U.S. Military Academy at West Point—not because he had suddenly decided on a soldier's life, but because it was a way to get a free college-level education that could lead to law school. Once he was at West Point, however, Pershing seemed to take to the military life: He became class president and senior captain in charge of cadets, the highest student position at the academy. He developed a reputation as a leader—and also as a strict disciplinarian.

First Assignments

Pershing left West Point in 1886 and went to New Mexico as a second lieutenant in the Sixth Cavalry Regiment in the U.S. Army. Just before he arrived, the Sixth had captured the Apache chief Geronimo (1829–1909), who had been notorious for eluding capture, but Pershing's four years in New Mexico were mostly spent in routine patrols.

In December 1890, Pershing and the Sixth Cavalry went to South Dakota to help suppress the Ghost Dance Rebellion, which involved Native American leader Sitting Bull (c. 1831–1890) and the Sioux tribe. However, Pershing arrived too late for the historic shooting of Sitting Bull and the massacre at Wounded Knee. He took part in only one skirmish, at Little Grass Creek on January 1.

In the fall of 1891, Pershing became a military instructor at the University of Nebraska and also taught remedial mathematics. He even found time to obtain the law degree he had long dreamed of; he considered abandoning the military for a career in law but decided against it.

Pershing stood out at the university as commandant of cadets. He took an undisciplined group of uninterested students and, in the words of the university chancellor, quoted by Frank Vandiver in *Black Jack,* transformed the group into "the best cadet corps outside of West Point." In less than a year, Pershing's cadets, later known as the Pershing Rifles, were able to win a national drill competition at Omaha, Nebraska.

From 1895 to 1896, Pershing commanded a unit of black soldiers in the Tenth Cavalry in Montana. He distinguished himself there by marching several hundred Cree Native Americans hundreds of miles into Canada. A year later, Pershing returned to West Point as an instructor but spent a very unsatisfactory year there. The cadets did not respond well to his strictness about how they marched, saluted, stood to attention, and dressed. In later years, too, Pershing would be criticized for what some saw as excessive attention to such matters. The cadets gave Pershing the silent treatment and also gave him a nickname that they intended as an insult: "Black Jack," referring to the fact that he had previously commanded black soldiers.

Cuba, the Philippines, and Pancho Villa

When the Spanish-American War broke out in 1898, Pershing managed to get himself sent to Cuba as the quartermaster (officer in charge of supplies) of the Tenth Cavalry. (War was declared by the United States on Spain because of a conflict over Cuba.) In Cuba, he won praise for his actions during the attack on San Juan Hill. According to Frank Vandiver in *Black Jack,* the colonel of Pershing's regiment told Pershing: "You were the coolest and bravest man I ever saw under fire in my life."

After Cuba, Pershing transferred to the Philippines, where he became known for suppressing uprisings on the island of Mindanao. He was made a captain and especially won fame for his march around Lake Lanao and his capture of the Moro (Muslim Filipino) stronghold at Bacolod in 1903. Three years later, President Theodore Roosevelt (1858–1919) promoted Pershing over the heads of 862 more senior officers to make him the youngest brigadier general in the army.

After serving as an observer in the Russo-Japanese War, Pershing returned to the Philippines and in 1909 to become military commander and civil governor of the Moro province. During the next four years, he introduced a minimum wage and price controls, started new schools and newspapers,

encouraged agricultural innovations, and provided new medical facilities. He also fought two more notable battles against hostile Moros, one at Bud Dajo and the other at Mount Bagsak.

In 1914, Pershing returned to the United States and was sent to El Paso, Texas, to guard against border raids by Mexicans. In March 1916, one such raid by Pancho Villa (1878–1923) killed seventeen Americans, and President

John J. Pershing riding a horse across a river in Mexico while searching for Pancho Villa, the leader of a band of Mexican border raiders. *Photograph courtesy of the National Archives and Records Administration.*

Woodrow Wilson (1856–1924) ordered Pershing to lead a "Punitive Expedition" into Mexico to capture Villa and break up his bands. Pershing spent the next eleven months in Mexico with more than ten thousand troops, but never caught Villa, though he did disperse one of Villa's bands.

World War I

Soon after the United States declared war on Germany on April 6, 1917, Wilson chose Pershing to command the American forces in Europe. At first the British and French were ecstatic over America's entry into the war, but they soon became impatient with Pershing's decision to delay committing American troops to battle. They pressed him to send U.S. soldiers to join British and French forces as soon as the Americans arrived. But Pershing wanted to train his troops first and then assemble them into an American army fighting under American command, not under the command of British or French generals.

Except for sending some American battalions to quiet parts of the front to get some experience in the trenches, Pershing did not allow American troops into combat all through 1917 and the first months of 1918. He was not inactive during this time, however. He set up training schools for officers and constructed a general staff divided into five sections, dealing with such matters as censorship and intelligence (spying), supplies and transport of troops, strategic studies, and training. He also established a general purchasing board to obtain supplies in Europe rather than relying entirely on what could be shipped from America.

After the Germans began a major offensive in March 1918, Pershing finally agreed to allow some American troops to fight on a temporary basis under British and French command. Then, in August 1918, Pershing was able to create the U.S. First Army. This army drove the Germans out of Saint-Mihiel in mid-September, and at the end of the month they launched the major American offensive of the war, in the Meuse-Argonne region. The offensive was not successful at first, but with a very high number of casualties, the Americans finally made a breakthrough on November 1. Ten days later the armistice (peace treaty) was signed, ending the war.

Controversies Surrounding the AEF

There are three major controversies surrounding the American Expeditionary Forces (AEF). Two of them are closely connected: First, should Pershing have waited as long as he did to send Americans into combat? Second, was he right to insist on creating an independent American army instead of funneling American troops into British and French regiments?

The British and French told Pershing that troops were needed immediately, or the war might be lost. They also said it would be better to integrate American troops into experienced Allied armies rather than have them led by inexperienced American commanders. Pershing argued that the Americans needed to be trained before being thrown into battle. He said they would fight better if they could retain their identity as an American army and have national pride to motivate them. He also expressed concern over language difficulties if the Americans fought under French command. And he did not have faith in the Allied commanders, who had led an unsuccessful war effort for three years and who, to him, seemed too attached to trench warfare. Who was right? Pershing mostly got his way, and the war was not lost—but some wonder if it might have been won sooner if the Americans had joined the fight more quickly.

The third controversy is over how well the Americans fought and how good a job Pershing did. According to Richard Goldhurst in *Pipe Clay and Drill,* "Pershing . . . brought to the American army unsuspected managerial and organizational skills, which enabled it to fight at the crest of its potential proficiency." But according to James Rainey, quoted by James Cooke in *Pershing and His Generals,* "The AEF succeeded not because of imaginative operations and tactics nor because of qualitative superiority, but by smothering German machine guns with American flesh."

In a way, these two views coincide, suggesting that if Pershing is to get credit for the victory, it is not because he excelled in the traditional military realms of tactics and strategy, but because he was a good enough manager to put more American troops on the battlefield than the Germans could handle.

Pershing argued against the armistice. He wanted the fighting to continue until the Germans surrendered unconditionally (allowing no compromises for Germany). He feared that otherwise Germany would someday threaten Europe again. During World War II (1939–45) Pershing thought he had been proved right. According to the editors of the *Army Times* in *The Yanks Are Coming,* Pershing made this comment in 1944: "If we had gone to Berlin then [in 1918], we would not be going there now."

Fading Away

Like victorious commanders after other wars, Pershing harbored presidential ambitions. But he did poorly in two primaries in 1920 and was never seriously considered as a candidate. Instead, he had to be content with the title "General of the Armies," which Congress conferred on him as a reward for the victory. He also became the army's chief of staff, a position he held until retiring in 1924.

In retirement, Pershing worked on his memoirs, finally publishing them in 1931. They are generally regarded as useful but lacking in excitement: He never did acquire a way with words. But the book did win a Pulitzer Prize in history. Pershing was in ill health the last several years of his life and stayed at the Walter Reed Hospital from 1941 until his death on July 15, 1948.

For More Information

Books

Cooke, James J. *Pershing and His Generals: Command and Staff in the AEF.* Westport, Conn.: Praeger, 1997.

Editors of the *Army Times. The Yanks Are Coming: The Story of General John J. Pershing.* New York: Putnam, 1960.

Goldhurst, Richard. *Pipe Clay and Drill: John J. Pershing: The Classic American Soldier.* New York: Reader's Digest, 1977.

Smith, Gene. *Until the Last Trumpet Sounds: The Life of General of the Armies John J. Pershing.* New York: Wiley, 1998.

Smythe, Donald. *Pershing: General of the Armies.* Bloomington: Indiana University Press, 1986.

Vandiver, Frank E. *Black Jack: The Life and Times of John J. Pershing.* 2 vols. College Station: Texas A&M University Press, 1977.

Films

Why America Will Win. Directed by Richard Stanton. Fox Film Corp., 1918. Silent film.

Web sites

Leach, Joseph. "Lafayette, We Are Here!" *The US Army in World War One.* [Online] http://www.grunts.net/wars/20thcentury/ww1/wearehere.html (accessed May 2001).

"The Life of General John J. Pershing." *Pershing Rifles National Headquarters.* [Online] http://www.unl.edu/prifles/life.htm (accessed May 2001).

Henri-Philippe Pétain

April 24, 1856
Cauchy-a-la-Tour, France
July 23, 1951
Port-Joinville, France

Military and political leader

"The irony of Pétain's life is that if he had died in 1939, at the ripe age of 83, he would be honorably remembered today as the hero of Verdun. . . . Instead . . . Pétain chose to become the symbol of France. . . . but it is the France of 1940 that he symbolizes: broken, confused, exhausted, and tarnished with the shame of collaboration."

—From David A. Bell, The New Republic, *January 28, 1985.*

Henri-Philippe Pétain.

Henri-Philippe Pétain had already lived a full life before historic events made him first a hero and then a traitor to the homeland he had loved and served. World War I broke out in Europe as Pétain was nearing the age of sixty and thinking of retirement from his military career. He postponed retirement to lead his troops, and his victories made the people of France love him. Decades later, as World War II (1939–45) raged, France again called on the aging Pétain, and he became premier (position like that of prime minister) of a French republic at war against Hitler's Germany. Positive the Germans could not be defeated, Pétain made a peace with the Germans—a peace that many called surrender. He not only allowed the Germans to occupy France, but his government cooperated with and helped the Germans. Many French citizens could not and still cannot forgive Pétain for this.

From Peasant to Soldier

Henri-Philippe Omer Pétain was born on April 24, 1856, the son of peasant farmers who had lived for centuries in the small village of Cauchy-a-la-Tour in northern France.

His young mother died shortly after the birth of her fifth child, when Pétain was only a year old. By the time Pétain was three, his father had remarried, but Pétain's stepmother was cold to her stepchildren, and Pétain spent much of his childhood living in his grandparents' house, right next door to his own. He was closest to two relatives on his mother's side: his uncle, who was a teacher, and his great-uncle, a priest who in his youth had been a soldier under French emperor Napoléon Bonaparte (1769–1821).

In 1867, Pétain became a student at the school where his uncle taught, the Collège Saint-Bertin. The little town of Saint-Omer, where the school was located, also was home base for a battalion of light-infantry soldiers, and young Pétain was impressed by the uniformed lieutenants he saw there. He decided he would be a soldier himself, a member of the light infantry. After he finished at Saint-Bertin, he spent a year at the more advanced Collège AlbertleGrand, then two years at the Special Military School of Saint-Cyr near Paris, graduating as a second lieutenant in 1878.

Pétain served actively for almost ten years, then enrolled in the École Supérieure de la Guerre (War College) for advanced military training. He was a hardworking student and dedicated soldier, but he did not have either the driving ambition or the flashy style that might have led to quick promotions. His climb up the military ranks was slow. Though he was handsome and a success at social events, his fellow officers often found him cold and unpleasant. During his career, he was sent to various French military bases and also returned to the War College several times to teach military strategy.

Pétain received praise and promotion for his work as a teacher. Influenced by the battles he had studied at the military school at Saint-Cyr, he developed a strategy for modern warfare. Because more powerful guns and artillery weapons were continually being developed, Pétain was convinced that these weapons should be used not for fierce attacks, but for a powerful defense, behind strong fortifications. Many disagreed with Pétain's defensive approach to warfare, including the commander of the War College, Ferdinand Foch (1851–1929).

Henri-Philippe Pétain salutes as German prisoners pass during a lull in the bloody battle of Verdun in 1916. *Reproduced by permission of AP/Wide World Photos.*

A War Hero

Pétain's defensive strategy would prove to be a success at an important time: When World War I began, Pétain was promoted from colonel to brigadier general and given command of an infantry division in the north of France. He used artillery and fortifications for his defensive approach to battle, and his tactics were successful. One of his most famous victories came at the town of Verdun, where Pétain's troops turned back a German offensive in 1916.

As the war dragged on, some French soldiers became unhappy and mistrustful of the men who were leading them. They began to mutiny, that is, they refused to follow their officers' orders. The soldiers who served under Pétain, however, loved and respected him because he was concerned about their welfare; he planned his strategies carefully to avoid casualties. In 1918, Pétain was appointed commander in chief of the army, in the hopes that he could control the rebellious soldiers. He punished some of the leaders of the mutinies, but he also made improvements in the soldiers' food and made sure they had breaks from battle so they could rest and recover. In 1918, Pétain was honored with the high rank of marshal of France. The men who had served under him would be his strongest supporters for the rest of his life.

World War I ended in 1918, but Pétain was not to remain at peace for long. In 1925, he went to Morocco to lead the joint Spanish-French army that fought against Moroccan rebel Abd elKrim. After that, Pétain finally did retire from active military duty, but he continued to serve the government as marshal of France and as inspector general of air defense. In 1934 he was appointed minister of war, and in 1939 he went to Spain as an ambassador to the government of dictator Francisco Franco.

Collaborator!

In 1940, with the world once more at war, Pétain was called back to France. The heavily fortified defenses that had been Pétain's strategy during World War I had not worked against the Germans this time, and France was being overwhelmed by German troops. At the age of eighty-four, Pétain was made vice-premier of France in the hopes that, as a beloved war hero, he could encourage the French people to resist the German invasion.

But Pétain did not believe that France could stop the Germans. On June 16, 1940, he became premier of the republic and made an agreement with Germany to stop the fighting. While the Germans occupied much of France by actively moving troops in, Pétain became the head of a new occupational government (a government controlled by a foreign military force), with its headquarters in the town of Vichy. In an effort to gain the French people better treatment from German occupiers, Pétain's government collaborated with the Germans. In wartime, collaboration means supporting and working together with the enemy. The Vichy government agreed to assist the Germans by rounding up French Jews and sending them to concentration camps; it also agreed to pay large amounts of money to the German government and send French workers to Germany. Though Pétain later insisted that he cooperated with the Germans because it was the only way to save France, many people think that he sym-

The Long, Slow Victory at Verdun

The bloody Battle of Verdun began on February 21, 1916, when German troops attacked the fortress town of Verdun, hoping to force the French army to waste precious lives and supplies defending the town. The battle was the longest of the war, lasting three hundred days and resulting in eight hundred thousand killed or wounded.

Verdun, in the north of France, had been a center of trade and transportation since the days when the Roman Empire ruled France. Close to the German border and equipped with fortifications, Verdun came to symbolize France's protection from German attack. But when the German army, descended on Verdun, the French forces could not hold them back. Within a few days the Germans had captured the nearby forts of Douaumont and Hardaumont. It seemed impossible to stop their advance.

Desperate to defend Verdun and protect the rest of France, Marshal Joseph Joffre, commander in chief of the French army, sent for a general who specialized in defensive maneuvers, Philippe Pétain. Pétain reinforced the town's defenses and called in constant supplies of new troops to replace those who were tired and battered by the fighting. He improved and protected the road leading south from Verdun so that troops and supplies could reach the battle.

"They shall not pass!" This was Pétain's promise to the French at Verdun, and he kept it. Pétain's armies stopped the German advance and lifted the mood of the entire country by holding the fortress at Verdun. However, the battle raged on, and it was not until December that the French regained all the territory around Verdun that had been lost to the Germans.

pathized with the Nazis and wished to help them win the war. (The Nazis were a German political movement led by Adolf Hitler that promoted racism and the expansion of state power.)

When the Allied forces attacked the Germans in France on June 6, 1944, Pétain left France and fled to Switzerland. Once the war was over, he was brought back to his homeland and, at eighty-nine years old, tried for treason. He was convicted and sentenced to death, but Charles de Gaulle, the new leader of France, reduced Pétain's sentence to life imprisonment. Already a very old man, Pétain, once the glorious war hero, spent the last years of his life in a prison on the island of Yeu. He died on July 23, 1951.

For More Information

Books

Griffiths, Richard. *Pétain: A Biography of Marshal Philippe Pétain of Vichy.* Garden City, NY: Doubleday, 1972.

Lottman, Herbert R. *Pétain, Hero or Traitor: The Untold Story.* New York: William Morrow, 1985.

Smith, Gene. *The Ends of Greatness: Haig, Pétain, Rathenau, and Eden: Victims of History.* New York: Crown, 1990.

Web sites

"Henri Pétain, French General." *Museum of Tolerance Online Multimedia Learning Center.* [Online] http://motlc.wiesenthal.com/pages/t060/t06012.html (accessed April 2001).

"Pétain, Henri-Phillippe Benomi Omer Joseph." [Online] http://www.historybookshop.com/articles/people/soldiersmilitary/petainhenri.asp (accessed March 2001).

Manfred von Richthofen

May 2, 1892
Breslau, Germany (now Wroc_aw, Poland)
April 21, 1918
Shot down over Vaux Kamsur Somme, France

Aviator and military leader

"The battle now taking place on all Fronts has become dreadfully serious; there is nothing left of the 'lively, merry war,' as our deeds were called in the beginning. Now we must arm ourselves against despair."

—From Manfred von Richthofen, The Red Fighter Pilot; quoted from http://www.richthofen.com; translated by J. Ellis Barker.

Manfred von Richthofen.
Reproduced by permission of AP/Wide World Photos, Inc.

The short, intense life of Baron Manfred von Richthofen is perhaps a testament to one of the many great tragedies of war: Too many of its heroes die young. An enthusiastic sportsman in childhood, Richthofen became a skilled and deadly hunter of men as a German fighter pilot during World War I. A dedicated soldier, he helped his country's cause with his many victories in the air. He was a dramatic hero who would inspire German troops in two world wars and earn respect even from his enemies.

An Unwilling Cadet

Manfred von Richthofen was born on May 2, 1892, into an aristocratic family. Both of his parents were descended from landowners, gentlemen farmers who were not inclined to go to war. However, Richthofen's father, Albrecht, had chosen a military career and achieved the rank of major. He took his military duties seriously and chose a military career for his oldest son, Manfred, as well.

Von Richthofen was the second child of four. He was born into a comfortable life in an area of northeastern Germany that today is part of Poland. Von Richthofen was an athletic youth who especially excelled in hunting and horseback riding. He was taught at home by tutors until he was nine years old; then he was sent to a school near his home for a year. When von Richthofen was eleven, his father sent him away to a military school in the town of Wahlstatt. Von Richthofen did not want to go, but he had to obey his father's wishes.

As a cadet in military school, von Richthofen continued to demonstrate his skill at all sports but barely scraped by in his schoolwork. He had little interest in his classes, did not get along with his schoolmates, and did only enough work to pass. Six years later, when he entered the Royal Prussian Military Academy near Berlin in 1909, von Richthofen finally began to enjoy the military life. He still triumphed at athletics, and he was starting to enjoy working and competing with his comrades. In 1911, he graduated from the academy and entered the Prussian cavalry, earning the rank of lieutenant in 1912.

From Horseback to the Pilot's Seat

Von Richthofen's lifelong love of horseback riding, along with his energy and enthusiasm, made him a natural cavalry officer. In the years before the war, his days consisted mainly of riding patrols along the Polish border and riding his own horses in races during his off-duty hours. When Germany entered World War I in August 1914, von Richthofen's cavalry unit, the Uhlan Regiment, was called into action to aid in the German attack on Belgium and Luxembourg and to fight in the first battle of Verdun in France.

It soon became apparent, however, that troops on horses were not going to hold their traditional place of importance in this modern war: Artillery was used to attack, and deep trenches were constantly being dug for defense. Von Richthofen and his men were soon off their horses and spending endless hours huddling in muddy trenches while the enemy fired shells at them. Life in the trenches was both boring and terrifying, and von Richthofen began to look for a more active way to spend the war. He sent a request to his general to be transferred to the *Fliegertruppe* (air service).

At first von Richthofen did not plan to pilot planes because he thought that flight training would take too long.

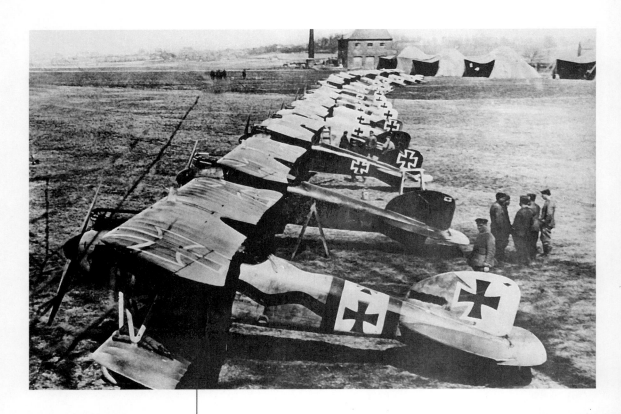

A view of "the Flying Circus," the squadron with which the Red Baron flew.
Reproduced by permission of Hulton Getty/Archive Photos, Inc.

So, in May 1915, he began his flight career as an observer, sitting beside the pilot on a bomber plane and gathering information to be used in future attacks. Soon, however, his impulsive nature won out, and he longed to take control and fly his own missions, not in the heavy bomber planes, but in the lightweight, fast, and fragile fighter planes. He persuaded a friend to teach him to fly, and after only twenty-four hours of flight training, he made his first solo flight. Though he crashed upon landing, he had learned from his years on horseback not to give up when thrown. He continued to train until 1916, when he was assigned to a fighter squadron. He made his first kill as pilot of a fighter plane on September 17, 1916.

The Red Baron

An able hunter on the ground, von Richthofen became a skilled hunter in the air as well. Within a few months, he had shot down ten enemy planes, the number required for a German pilot to be called an "ace." Each day he eagerly flew up into battle, honing his skills in pursuit and marksmanship. The new young ace reveled in his victories. He collected souvenirs from each plane he shot down and bought a small engraved trophy to celebrate each of his kills. His victories made him so conceited that his superior officers began to worry that he would become sloppy in his flying. However, von Richthofen never became careless, but only more and more skilled at his deadly work. His cocky attitude eventually subsided a bit as he witnessed the deaths of many of his friends and comrades.

In November 1916, von Richthofen added to his fame by shooting down Major Lanoe Hawker, a famed British ace pilot. On January 16, 1917, von Richthofen was decorated with the highest German war medal, the *Ordre Pour la Merite,* or as it was nicknamed, the Blue Max. In the same month, he was given command of his own *Jagdstaffel* (fighter squadron). *Jagdstaffel* 11 was an unsuccessful squadron in need of a strong leader, and von Richthofen immediately began to whip them into shape. The squadron's air victories increased dramatically, but no one had more kills than the new commander.

Von Richthofen counted up his kills as enthusiastically as any sports fan keeping score. It was around this time that he painted his fighter plane bright red. He wanted it to be recognized from the ground, so that ground troops would not accidentally fire on it—and so that observers on the ground would give him credit for the planes he shot down. Other pilots in his squadron took up the practice of painting bright colors on their planes, and soon the squadron earned the fitting nickname, "the Flying Circus." The British called the squadron commander the "red baron" or the "red knight," and the French called him "le petit rouge" (little red). Both respected and feared the red plane's relentless pilot was adding several kills to his record nearly every day.

In April 1917, von Richthofen was promoted to captain. He was extremely valuable to the German army—not only for his combat skills, but also for his dashing and heroic image, which made an excellent propaganda (the spreading of ideas or information to further or damage a cause) tool to raise German morale. The few times he took leave to rest from the exhausting action at the front, he was pressured by those in charge of military propaganda to write the story of his adven-

From Films to Cartoons: The Red Baron Lives On

For decades, World War I flying aces have captured the imagination of novelists, filmmakers, and dreamers everywhere. Perhaps it is because of the pilots' flashy outfits, with leather helmets and coveralls, silk scarves, and fur coats; perhaps it is because of their tiny, delicate, yet fierce airplanes; perhaps it is because of their youth and their careless, smiling courage in the face of death. However, of all the daring aces, Baron Manfred von Richthofen, Germany's ace of aces, is probably the best known.

In some cases, his name merely means romance. An American frozen food company uses the name Red Baron on its frozen pizza, and their commercials feature a handsome leather-helmeted pilot who turns up for dinner when his brand of pizza is cooked. In other cases, his nickname represents danger and a bloodthirsty inclination to kill: In the 1994 film *Revenge of the Red Baron,* for example, the Baron's ghost returns to stalk the descendants of the British pilot who killed von Richthofen in 1918.

Perhaps the most famous and touching tribute to the German ace is found in *Peanuts,* a comic strip created in 1950 by Charles Schulz (1922–2000). One of the strip's most endearing characters is Snoopy, a philosophical beagle whose favorite game involves pretending to be a World War I flying ace on the trail of the Red Baron. "Drat you, Red Baron!" Snoopy howls, shaking his fist as the German pilot escapes again and echoing exactly the mix of frustration and grudging admiration that Allied pilots must have felt when they confronted the Red Baron in the sky.

tures. He was paraded before crowds of cheering admirers, and parties were given in his honor by the leaders of the country. Though von Richthofen had sought fame and recognition, he was uncomfortable with such ceremonies; he soon wanted to leave so he could go hunting at his home in Breslau before returning to the front to shoot down enemy planes.

On July 6, 1917, shortly after his fifty-seventh kill, von Richthofen himself was shot down. He survived the crash of his plane behind German lines and was rescued and taken to a German military hospital with a serious gunshot wound in his head. Though he recovered enough to return to duty by August 16, it is probable that his wound never really healed. He fought the pain and continued flying, sealing his title as "ace of aces" by shooting down a total of eighty enemy planes. In the winter of 1917, his memoirs, *Der Rote Kampfflieger* (*The Red Fighter Pilot*) were published. His book was distributed to German infantry soldiers to encourage them to fight bravely.

On April 21, 1918, von Richthofen was in a fight against a British pilot. Pushing the limits as usual, von Richthofen chased the British pilot farther and faster than the rules said he should. As a result, von Richthofen's plane was shot down over the Somme River in France, and he was killed in the crash. He was buried with honor and given a military funeral by the British troops who recovered his body.

For More Information

Books

Gibbons, Floyd Phillips. *The Red Knight of Germany: The Story of Baron von Richthofen, Germany's Great War Bird.* Garden City, NY: Doubleday, 1927.

Kilduff, Peter. *The Illustrated Red Baron.* London: Arms and Armour Press, 1999.

Kilduff, Peter. *Richthofen: Beyond the Legacy of the Red Baron.* New York: John Wiley and Sons, 1994.

Wright, Nicolas. *The Red Baron.* New York: McGrawHill, 1977.

Web sites

"The Red Baron." [Online] http://www.briggsenterprises.com/bluemax/ (accessed April 2001).

Richthofen, Manfred von. *The Red Fighter Pilot* (online text of *Der Rote Kampfflieger,* 1917; translated into English by J. Ellis Barker, 1918). [Online] http://www.richthofen.com (accessed April 2001).

Eddie Rickenbacker

October 8, 1890
Columbus, Ohio
July 23, 1973
Miami, Florida

Aviator and businessman

"In his long, crowded life Captain Edward V. Rickenbacker was a dauntless fighter pilot, a spellbinding orator, an international agent, a pioneer of commercial aviation and spokesman for all the airlines, a self-improver to rival Benjamin Franklin. . . ."

—From Finis Farr,
Rickenbacker's Luck:
An American Life.

Eddie Rickenbacker.
Reproduced by permission of
AP/Wide World Photos, Inc.

Eddie Rickenbacker is perhaps best remembered as the young World War I flying ace, pictured leaning against a plane in coveralls and a leather helmet, smiling with cocky self-assurance. Though he had countless brushes with death and may have seemed the kind of hero likely to die young, Rickenbacker survived two wars and lived to be eighty-two years old. During his lifetime, he saw the birth of the automobile and the airplane. He fell in love with those technologies, worked in the industries that produced them, and played a major part in making both automobile and airplane travel accessible to the average American.

First-Generation American

Edward Rickenbacher was born in Columbus, Ohio, on October 8, 1890, and spent his early life hard at work in the American Midwest. His parents, William and Elizabeth Rickenbacher, had met in Ohio, where they each had come to from Switzerland in the 1870s. They married and had eight children, one of whom died while still a baby. Their third son was named Edward, though he would always be known to friends as "Rick." In later years, Eddie "Rick" Rickenbacher would take the middle name Vernon and change the spelling of his last name so it would look and sound less German and more "American."

William Rickenbacher was a stern and serious man who worked hard running a construction business. Elizabeth had a deep love of art and poetry and tried to show her children the gentler side of life. The family was quite poor, and young Eddie Rickenbacker was introduced to adult responsibility early. To help support his family, he began working odd jobs when he was seven. He was a tough, adventurous child who smoked cigarettes at the age of five and ran with a group of pals called the Horsehead Gang. His first language was the Swiss German his parents spoke at home, and he was teased and bullied at school because of his accent. In those fights, Rickenbacker learned to stand up for himself.

A Love of Speed

Life did not get easier: In 1904 Rickenbacker's father was killed on the job, and even more responsibility fell on Rickenbacker's young shoulders. He went from job to job, from a steel mill to a beer factory to a bowling alley, looking for a career that was more than a way to bring in money. He was fascinated by the newly invented automobile and decided to take a correspondence course in mechanical engineering. He soon got a job at Frayer Miller, an auto plant in Columbus. It was there he met Lee Frayer, an auto manufacturer and racecar driver.

Frayer introduced Rickenbacker to the world of auto racing, and soon his new employee was hooked. First as a mechanic, then a driver, he participated in races all over the United States from 1906 to 1917, setting a world speed record at 134 miles per hour in 1917. He drove on tracks located in New York to those in California, making thousands of dollars by winning races and earning a reputation as one of the world's most daring racecar drivers.

A Call to War

Rickenbacker's daring would soon be put to a greater test. In 1914, war had broken out in Europe, and Americans whose parents had recently come from European countries felt

American pilot Eddie
Rickenbacker poses in front
of the plane he used to
shoot down many German
planes during World War I.
*Reproduced by permission
of Hulton Getty/Archive
Photos, Inc.*

especially touched by the war. When the United States entered the war in 1917, Rickenbacker enlisted and was sent to Europe to be a driver on General John Joseph Pershing's staff. However, Rickenbacker had no intention of spending the war behind the wheel of a jeep. He wanted to fly fighter planes, and by August 1917, he had managed to get into flight training for the army air corps in Tours, France. He was assigned to the Ninety-fourth Aero Pursuit Squadron, also called the "Hat in the Ring" Squadron because of the symbol of a top hat in a circle that was painted on its planes. The hat in the ring represented an old custom of throwing a hat into a boxing ring to challenge an opponent to a fight.

On April 29, 1918, Rickenbacker shot down his first German plane. His reputation for courage and boldness spread quickly throughout the air corps and at home in the United States. After shooting down five planes, a pilot received the title "ace," and Rickenbacker was soon being called "America's Ace of Aces." He flew dozens of missions over France and Ger-

Rickenbacker the Psychic?

During his lifetime Eddie Rickenbacker saw great changes in society and technology. He saw transportation progress from horsedrawn wagons to superhighways and supersonic jets. He witnessed the development of the telephone, the television, and the early computer. Perhaps because he saw such tremendous change, he loved to wonder and predict what changes the future might bring.

The last chapter of Rickenbacker's autobiography, published in 1967, is filled with his predictions of the technological advances he thought could happen within fifty years. In the future, Rickenbacker said, airplanes would carry a thousand passengers or more and travel at speeds of up to five thousand miles per hour. Most individuals would own helicopters, and cities would have central heliports where commuters could land. Those who did not fly helicopters to work might wear rocket belts, which would allow them to fly without a vehicle. New engines, based on the jet engine, would be invented to power automobiles. The sky would be filled with space stations that would offer regular flights to other planets as well as shuttles back to Earth.

Rickenbacker came closer to reality in his financial predictions. In the future, he guessed, money for payments and investments would not have to be physically transported from place to place; it would be transferred instantly through the use of electronics and television screens. Bills and orders for products also could be instantly sent and received in this way. Though the world has yet to see rocket belts for sale, Rickenbacker's instanttransfer machines bear an amazing resemblance to modern computers and fax machines. As for his other predictions—the plane Rickenbacker flew in World War I would probably have seemed just as unbelievable to Rickenbacker's grand-parents as a thousandpassenger jet seems to people at the beginning of the twenty-first century.

many, often going up twice a day. He eventually commanded the Ninety-fourth, and the squadron shot down a total of six-tynine enemy planes. Rickenbacker reached a personal total of twenty-six kills on November 10, 1918, just one day before the end of the war. For his bravery and success in the war effort, France rewarded Rickenbacker in 1918 with the Croix de Guerre (Cross of War), a high military honor. He also received the U.S. Medal of Honor, but it was not awarded until 1930.

A Captain of Industry

After World War I and II, Eddie Rickenbacker went on to become one of the great leaders of American industry. *Photograph courtesy of The Library of Congress.*

Back in the United States after the war, Rickenbacker married a woman of society lady named Adelaide Frost and began a new life as a family man. He started the Rickenbacker Motor Company in Detroit, Michigan, to manufacture his own cars, but in 1926 the factory closed. He worked for Cadillac Motors and General Motors for short periods, then renewed his interest in airplanes and went to work for several different aircraft companies. Just as in his youth, Rickenbacker seemed to be searching for the perfect career. In 1934, he accepted the job of general manager at Eastern Air Lines. The company had been newly formed from Eastern Air Transport and was not doing well, losing $1.5 million in 1934. Under Rickenbacker's management, however, things began to turn around. In 1938, Eastern made $38,000 in profits, and Rickenbacker was made president. From then until 1963, when he retired as president, Eastern made a profit every year, proving Rickenbacker's talents as a manager and businessman.

By the end of the 1930s, the United States was once again approaching war, but this time Rickenbacker was not enthusiastic. An extreme political conservative, Rickenbacker was sympathetic to many of the ideas of the Nazi Party in Germany, and he did not think the United States should get involved in the war. (The Nazis were a political party led by Adolf Hitler that promoted racism and the expansion of state power.) However, when war came, he did not refuse to serve his country. He acted as a representative of the secretary of war, traveling to various military bases as an inspector and advisor. On one of these trips, flying from Honolulu, Hawaii, to New Guinea, the plane he was flying in crashed into the Pacific Ocean. Once again courage and endurance were demanded of the former flying ace. He and six other passengers drifted on a raft for twenty-three days before being rescued. With characteristic toughness, Rickenbacker rested only a few days after his rescue, then completed his mission.

In 1950, Rickenbacker's picture appeared on the cover of *Time* magazine, which honored him not only as a veteran of two world wars, but also as a leader of industry who helped shape modern air travel. Rickenbacker was revered by many for his heroic wartime actions and his sharp business sense, but he was criticized by others for his right-wing (conservative) political views. He was an active anti-communist and had disliked President Franklin Roosevelt's New Deal, a system of government aid that helped people financially during the Great Depression of the 1930s. Rickenbacker had racist attitudes toward blacks and Jews and believed that the only proper role for a woman was as a wife.

Rickenbacker was nevertheless a loving husband to Adelaide and a good father to their three sons. After his retirement, Rickenbacker and his wife moved to Florida. He died there in 1973, surrounded by his family.

For More Information

Books

Farr, Finis. *Rickenbacker's Luck: An American Life*. Boston: Houghton Mifflin, 1979.

Rickenbacker, Edward V. *Rickenbacker*. Englewood Cliffs, NJ: PrenticeHall, 1967.

Article

Halacy, Dan. "Rickenbacker: America's Ace of Aces." *Boys' Life,* December 1980, 38–43.

Web sites

"The Charmed Life of Eddie Rickenbacker." [Online] http://www.thehistorynet.com/AviationHistory/articles/1999/0199_text.htm (accessed April 2001).

Rickenbacker, Edward V. "Fighting the Flying Circus" (online version of Rickenbacker's memoirs). *War Times Journal.* [Online] http://www.richthofen.com/rickenbacker/ (accessed April 2001).

"Rickenbacker Papers: Historical Sketch of Eddie." *Auburn University Archives*. [Online] http://www.lib.auburn.edu/archive/flyhy/101/eddie.htm (accessed April 2001).

Alan Seeger

June 28, 1888
New York City, New York
July 4, 1916
Belloy-en-Santerre, France

Poet, soldier

I have a rendezvous
with Death
At some disputed
barricade,
When Spring comes back
with rustling shade
And appleblossoms
fill the air

. . . .

And I to my pledged
word am true,
I shall not fail that
rendezvous.

*From "I Have a Rendezvous
with Death," in Alan
Seeger, Poems.*

American poet Alan Seeger is best remembered for "I Have a Rendezvous with Death," a poem that foreshadowed Seeger's death in battle during World War I. Seeger lived a bohemian (unconventional) lifestyle in New York's Greenwich Village before moving to France in 1912. When war broke out in 1914, he was one of the first Americans to enlist in the French Foreign Legion (a branch of the French military open to foreigners). In letters to his family and to American periodicals, he expressed the idealism and courage of many young men of his generation who answered the call of duty in World War I. On the Fourth of July 1916, nearly a year before the United States entered the war, came Seeger's own death, as he fell in battle while trying to liberate a French village from the Germans. A collection of his works, *Poems,* was published in 1916 and included several dozen lyrics, odes, and sonnets. "I Have a Rendezvous with Death" is the only one that is well-known today.

A Privileged Childhood

Alan Seeger was born in New York City on June 28, 1888, the son of businessman Charles Louis Seeger and Elsie

Simmons Adams Seeger. Alan had an older brother and a younger sister. His father made a large fortune from sugar refineries in Mexico, so the family lived in comfortable circumstances on Staten Island, the most rural of the five boroughs of New York City. Alan's brother, a musicologist (a person who studies music as a field of research), was the father of Pete Seeger (1919–), activist and folksinger.

Alan Seeger got his education at prestigious private schools, such as the Staten Island Academy and the Horace Mann School in Manhattan. When he was twelve years old, the Seegers moved to Mexico City, and Alan helped his parents produce a family magazine they called the *Prophet*. The time he spent in Mexico later inspired him to write a number of poems that describe that country as a vivid and exotic land. In one of them, "An Ode to Antares," Seeger paints himself as a "fond romanticist" encountering a carefree environment where "The tropic sunset's bloom on cloudy piles / Cast out industrious cares with dreams of fabulous isles." In "Tezcotzinco," he imagines native people strolling through the gardens of an ancient Aztec king, their "Bare bodies beautiful, brown, glistening, / Decked with green plumes and rings of yellow gold." Seeger's health was not good, and his parents thought the high altitude of Mexico City was too difficult for him; so in 1902 the young man returned to the United States to enroll at the Hackley School in Tarrytown, New York. He then spent a year with a tutor in southern California before going back East to study at Harvard College, where he was editor of the *Harvard Monthly*. At Harvard, he became interested in Celtic literature, and he wrote many original poems as well as translations from Dante (1265–1321) and other classical writers.

Bohemian Lifestyle

Graduating from Harvard in 1910, Seeger returned to New York City and began associating with the bohemian and avant-garde (experimental; innovative) artists and writers who were then living in Greenwich Village. For a time, he shared an apartment with a Harvard classmate, John Reed (1887–1920), who later became an avid supporter of the revolution in Russia and of the Communist government that replaced the czar's rule there. (Communism is a system of government in which the state plans and controls the economy and a single party holds power with the goal of equally dividing all goods among the people.)

Ever a restless soul, Seeger thought that New York was too limiting for him, so in 1912 he moved to Paris. There he took up residence in the Latin Quarter with other expatriates (people who live in another country and sometimes give up their citizenship) from the United States and Europe. It was during this period that he wrote a collection of poems that he called *Juvenilia*. Seeger also enjoyed taking long hikes through the French countryside. In the summer of 1914, he visited London to try to find a publisher for *Juvenilia*. But then World War I broke out; he returned to France and became one of the first Americans to join the French Foreign Legion, a choice that fit his idealistic and risk-taking personality.

A Soldier in the French Foreign Legion

After basic training at Rouen, Seeger was assigned to Battalion C of the Second Regiment of the foreign legion, which was based at Toulouse in the south of France. From that city he wrote a letter to his mother in September 1914; an excerpt, quoted in the online "Letters and Diary of Alan Seeger," expresses the reasoning behind his commitment to fight for France: ". . . in this universe strife and sternness play as big a part as love and tenderness, and cannot be shirked by one whose will it is to rule his life in accordance with the cosmic forces he sees in play about him." In another letter from the same source, Seeger refused to think of the dangers of combat, instead describing the fighting in the most positive and idealistic of terms: "Every day, from the distance to the north, has come the booming of the cannon around Reims and the lines along the Meuse [River]. . . . But imagine how thrilling it will be tomorrow and the following days, marching toward the front."

The United States was not involved in World War I until 1917, but many American newspaper readers learned of the situation on the front lines through a series of letters Seeger wrote for the *New York Sun*. Painting a vivid picture of the loneliness of sentry duty or the experience of lying in the trenches as shells burst overhead, Seeger's accounts helped Americans understand the plight of the typical soldier caught up in a horrendous conflict. But for Seeger, fighting for a noble cause was an act of deep spiritual satisfaction. He wrote to his mother in

Minor Poets of World War I

As educated young men from across the United States and Canada joined the battles of World War I, they also joined in recording their feelings about the war, often in poetry. Though their work is not as acclaimed as that of Seeger or the famous British poets Wilfred Owen (1893–1918) and Siegfried Sassoon (1886–1967), two poets from North America have attracted attention because of their work.

Joyce Kilmer (1886–1918)

Once a staff writer for the *New York Times,* Joyce Kilmer is known primarily as the author of "Trees" ("I think that I shall never see / A poem lovely as a tree . . ."). He also wrote "The White Ships and the Red," a poem about the sinking of the Irish passenger ship *Lusitania.* German submarines sank the ship in 1915, an act of wartime aggression. Some of Kilmer's other poems about war are included in his third collection, *Main Street,* published in 1917, the same year he enlisted in the U.S. Army. He was killed in action in France in July 1918 and buried near Seringes.

John McCrae (1872–1918)

This Canadian physician had written a few poems during the Boer War (1899–1902) in South Africa, where he served as a medical officer in the British army. He performed similar military duties during World War I and died in France of an infection he contracted while serving there. He is remembered for a fifteen-line poem called "In Flanders Fields," which appeared in *Punch,* the British magazine, on December 8, 1915. Its opening lines—"In Flanders fields, the poppies blow / Between the crosses row on row . . ."—evoke the image of World War I military cemeteries in Europe. Immortalized by McCrae's poem, the red poppy is still regarded as a symbol of veterans of that conflict.

July 1915, in a letter quoted in the online "Letters and Diary of Alan Seeger": "Whether I am on the winning or the losing side is not the point with me: it is being on the side where my sympathies lie that matters, and I am ready to see it through to the end. . . . [H]ad I the choice I would be nowhere else in the world than where I am." Seeger's letters also reveal how much he admired the French, who seemed to him far more sincere and passionate about their cause than the Germans did.

In the spring of 1916, Seeger took two months' leave from the foreign legion to recover from an attack of bronchitis. He visited Biarritz and Paris and arranged to have the manuscript of *Juvenilia* sent to him. He concluded that there was "much that was good in it, but much that was juvenile, too," and he decided he was "not so anxious to publish it as it stands." The collection was later published by Charles Scribner's Sons in an edition titled *Poems*. It included the contents of *Juvenilia,* four translations of classical Greek or Roman poems, and a group of twenty-three "Last Poems" written from the time of his enlistment until his death in 1916. "I Have a Rendezvous with Death" was included among these "Last Poems," as was "A Message to America," a rather controversial poem that called on the United States to unite under the leadership of Theodore Roosevelt (1858–1919), who wanted to lead troops in France but could not persuade President Woodrow Wilson (1856–1924) to let him do so.

Death on the Western Front

When Seeger returned to the front after his recovery from bronchitis, he participated in daring, sometimes dangerous enterprises, like wandering out at night, alone, toward the German trenches. Once he even stuck his calling card on the barbed wire surrounding the enemy's trenches, explaining his risky mission by quoting a line of poetry by Walt Whitman (1819–1892): "courting destruction with taunts, with invitations."

Among the poems Seeger wrote during this period was "Ode in Memory of the American Volunteers Fallen for France." Few remember this ode today, but William Archer, the Scottish critic who wrote the introduction to *Poems*, thought it was Seeger's best work, "the crown of the poet's achievement." In it, Seeger praises the French for accepting American volunteers like himself and making it possible for them to earn "that chance to live the life most free from stain / And that rare privilege of dying well."

On July 4, 1916, the 140th anniversary of U.S. independence, Seeger was granted the privilege he had described: Just twenty-eight years old, he was killed by machine-gun fire while trying to liberate the village of BelloyenSanterre. Nearly a year after Seeger's death, more of his work was published in an edition called *Letters and Diaries*. The United States had just entered World War I, and the publication of this collection gave American readers a personalized account of day-to-day life on foreign battlefields. Though Seeger's death may seem like a tragic loss, Seeger himself probably would not have seen it this way. In fact, in the introduction to *Poems,* William Archer wrote that "Of all the poets who died young, none has died so happily."

For More Information

Books

Moore, T. Sturge. *Some Soldier Poets*. New York: Harcourt, Brace and Hove, 1920.

Seeger, Alan. *Letters and Diaries*. New York: Charles Scribner's Sons, 1917.

Seeger, Alan. *Poems*. New York: Charles Scribner's Sons, 1916. Reprint, New York: AMS Press, 1973.

Weinstein, Irving. *Sound No Trumpet: The Life and Death of Alan Seeger*. New York: Crowell, 1967.

Web sites

"Letters and Diary of Alan Seeger." [Online] http://www.ukans.edu/~libsite/wwiwww/Seeger/Alan1.htm (accessed April 2001).

"Selected Poetry of Alan Seeger (1888–1916)." *Representative Poetry Online.* [Online] http://www.library.utoronto.ca/utel/rp/authors/seeger.html (accessed April 2001).

Richard Stumpf

Born 1892

German seaman

Richard Stumpf was an ordinary German soldier, but he wrote an extraordinary diary. Unlike the officers and politicians who wrote memoirs for publication, Stumpf only wrote for himself. Instead of writing so that the world would remember him well or to "set the record straight," Stumpf wrote to amuse and entertain himself, to vent his anger, and to record what he knew about the war. He wrote daily and sometimes hourly to stave off the boredom of being an enlisted seaman from 1914 to the end of World War I. His diary stands as the best description of the life of a regular enlisted German during the war and the collapse of the German Empire in 1918. No other account so accurately captures the little man's perspective. Stumpf's diary was the only personal history used by the Reichstag Investigating Committee in 1926 as it researched the causes of the two German navy mutinies (sailors not following the orders of their commanding officers) in 1917 and 1918 and the ensuing German revolution. (The Reichstag was Germany's lower legislative house.)

An Ordinary Sailor

As with most ordinary soldiers in history, little is known about Richard Stumpf's personal life. Born in 1892, Stumpf became a tinsmith and joined a Christian trade union. Stumpf was a devoted Catholic and, at the start of World War I, a self-proclaimed "fanatic patriot" with conservative political opinions. Stumpf joined the German navy in 1912, and according to his diary, he tried to live up to the example set by his father, who had spent thirty years as a professional soldier. Stumpf served as a seaman on the *Helgoland* for six years and was transferred to the *Wittelsbach* and then the *Lothringen* in 1918. He spent much of the war loading tons of coal, scraping paint, and doing tiresome military drills. He saw little action, and so his diary is composed of his attempts to make sense of his daily existence as an idle sailor and the stories and rumors he heard about distant battles. Although his life and thoughts during the war are known in great detail, almost nothing is known about him after the war. He moved to Nuremberg, Germany, to work as a tinsmith, but like many other enlisted men, he slipped into obscurity.

Stumpf did not present his diary to the public until 1926, when the Reichstag Investigating Committee began its investigation into the causes of the German revolution of 1918. He had never thought to publish the six large notebooks he had filled, but he felt compelled to share them with the committee as records of German sailors' experiences during the war. The committee was immediately impressed with Stumpf's work. His diary spanned the entire war, recording Stumpf's enthusiastic war fever at the onset, his boredom as the years wore on, and his growing anger at superiors who acted callously toward the enlisted men and seemed to live richly while he and his comrades survived on smaller and smaller rations. Interestingly, Stumpf's diary also recorded his transformation from an ardent supporter of the kaiser (the German term for emperor) to a mutineer. Furthermore, Stumpf's personal memoirs were written in such a way that they represented "all the thousands of sailors who never kept diaries of their own," according to Daniel Horn, who edited Stumpf's diary and translated it into English. Stumpf's broad knowledge of German, French, Russian, and British history and his keen observation made it possible for him to describe the experiences of thousands of unknown soldiers.

Strong Evidence

With Stumpf's diary as evidence, the committee could throw out the theory that the mutinies were caused by a propaganda campaign and subversive actions masterminded by radical socialists. (Socialism is a social system based on shared or government ownership and administration of the means of the production and distribution of goods.) According to Horn, Stumpf's diary provided the committee with unique information about "why the enlisted men of the German navy revolted against their officers, why Germany lost the war, why the Empire collapsed, and why it was overthrown by revolution." Stumpf's account proved that even the most patriotic enlisted men could not remain devoted to the war in the face of the terrible treatment they suffered. Stumpf pinned the downfall of Germany on the troops' "hunger and starvation" and "their mistreatment by the officers, and their intense desire for peace." Moreover, his diary revealed that most enlisted men had little knowledge of the activities carried on by radicals and no sympathy for them in any case.

At the beginning of the war, Stumpf related how life changed on board the *Helgoland,* the ship he was assigned to in 1912. During the first few months of the war, Stumpf wrote enthusiastically about Germany's victories on the Western Front, and he sounded optimistic about defeating the infamous British navy. But as the war wore on, he described the boredom of inactive duty and the anxious desire of the soldiers to battle their enemies. Importantly, he also noted the behavior of his superiors. "[O]fficers treat the common seaman with inconceivable cruelty," Stumpf wrote on November 8, 1915. "Each day twenty to thirty men are made to run around with their rifles. My greatest ambition in life is to get away from all this stupidity and harassment! Although I was happy when I entered the navy, I have now come to detest it!" Stumpf wrote that the crew was "constantly harassed by these petty pinpricks," and he described some of the silly rules that the enlisted men were forced to follow:

> [W]e are strongly forbidden under penalty of imprisonment to wear anything but a white uniform by day or night. (Note: The Captain has promised to punish any violators with five days of imprisonment.) Secondly, we are not allowed to bring coats, newspapers or books into the gun turrets. (To illustrate how insane this rule really is, it must be noted that we are not allowed to place our coats anywhere

else either.) Thirdly, the Captain gave two of the men seven days of arrest for failing to wear their life jackets. Fourthly, we are forbidden to hang our hammocks even where there are no guns. (I cannot fathom the reason behind this. Only deliberate nastiness could conceive of such a thing.)

Life On Board Ship

By 1916, life on board the *Helgoland* had deteriorated further. In September, Stumpf recorded the first mutinous behavior of German sailors. "On our ship we have ample cause for complaint and reflection," he wrote. "Our miserable food and ill-treatment had already resulted in open refusals to obey orders (on the part of the first division). Indeed our morale has deteriorated so badly that someone removed the safety pin from one of the guns and cut through one of the lines amidship [at the middle point of the ship between the bow and the stern]. Consequently all the guns are now guarded day and night. Although the identity of the culprit remains unknown, our food has improved remarkably. And after all, this was the aim of the action."

But things did not improve for long on Stumpf's ship. Within a month, he marked the anniversary of joining the navy with a gloomy entry: "Exactly four years ago today, I arrived here as a new recruit. At that time my heart was still filled with high hopes and expectations. I wanted to be a good, efficient sailor. I would never have thought it possible that so many obstacles would be placed in the way of my good intentions. Nevertheless, I had decided that I would allow nothing to deter me. I was determined not to abandon my principles, even for the navy. I now realize how badly I have failed. I encountered such a great lack of understanding and ill will on the part of my superiors that I was at last compelled to give up the struggle. I grew tired, embittered and resigned. I was forced to look on without complaint while men with decidedly inferior minds practiced the vilest cruelties." Stumpf noted that he himself refused to salute certain officers, even when he knew he would suffer punishment for his disobedience. Without remorse, Stumpf admitted that by that time he was regarded as a "Red" rather than the patriot he had always been.

On November 17, 1916, Stumpf described how little respect he had for the military system he once so admired.

Mutiny: Soldiers and Citizens Pushed to Despair

Feeling unfairly burdened by the stresses of the war effort, German sailors of the High Seas Fleet protested in August 1917, refusing to obey their superiors' orders. This first mutiny was quickly subdued when navy officials issued harsh punishment; but a second mutiny, in November 1918, inspired the German population and sparked the German revolution. That month, the enlisted sailors took over the German ships and naval bases at Wilhelmshaven and Kiel, ousting their superiors from power.

The sailors' success prompted German workers to rebel against the government. The German people wanted relief from wartime stresses: To supply the German military with weapons, food, and other supplies, they had worked long hours, had little to eat, and donated much of their personal savings to the war effort. Feeling that the kaiser and others in power had little regard for the wishes of common folk, workers revolted against the German monarchist state in 1918 and eventually established a new representative government.

Although the Germans succeeded in setting up a new government, they did not escape harsh punishment for their part in World War I. Germany reeled from the devastating aftereffects of the war. It had to give up the territory it held during the bloody battles, it had to send its enemies large parts of its sophisticated weaponry, and it was forced to pay extremely high sums to the Allied forces for damages. For the average person, life in Germany after the war was not much better than life during the war: Food was scarce; work was hard; pay was low. In the years to come, these conditions contributed to the rise of the Nazi Party, led by Adolf Hitler (1889–1945), and fueled tensions that would lead to a second world war in 1939.

"[M]y hatred for the navy keeps growing," he reported. "I now realize better than ever before, how stupid we really are to do all the work while those who merely look on get all the pay. We live in an unjust and evil world. Should the opportunity ever arise, I will be only too happy to make it better. Damn the officers! Never again shall they be allowed to drag us into war! Let them either practice some honorable profession or drop dead! They shall no longer earn a living from our stupidity and grow fat on our money." Stumpf was keenly aware that he was not the only German losing faith in the government and the upper classes. He observed the discontent of civilians as well as soldiers. In 1917, rations were cut throughout Germany, and Stumpf noted the news of workers' strikes in Berlin, Leipzig, and other cities. When two hundred thousand workers in Berlin left work demanding more food, he wondered if Germany would lose the war as a result of starvation. He was aware that the workers' strike in Leipzig involved demands for voting rights and withdrawal from the war. He also commented favorably about the workers' revolution in Russia at the time.

A Shift of Faith

Stumpf could no longer see how people like him, proletariats (people who own no property and who earn a living by working for wages), would benefit at all from the war. He had shifted from being a monarchist (supporter of the kaiser) and decided that a representational government like that found in America would be better for Germany. He grew angry at the German government for denying people the chance to represent themselves with a vote. "It almost makes me die for shame when I consider that even now our overconfident landed gentry [people of high social standing] deem it possible to deny the right to vote to the very people who protect their property with their lives," he raged. "Do the Conservatives think that they alone would have been capable of rolling back the invading Russian hordes? What a shame that we cannot lay down our arms for at least a day and allow the Indians and the New Zealanders [soldiers from the British colonies of India and New Zealand] to run amuck on the estates of the Junkers [wealthy German landowners]. Maybe that would make them understand why the working classes are much less interested in our victory than the propertied classes."

Others had similar reactions to the war, and Stumpf wrote often about the growing revolutionary feelings of the soldiers. "In truth no dark foreign powers are needed to drive the most patient and the most disciplined people in the world to desperation," Stumpf noted in November 1917. "I have often wished that our officers would carry their madness to such a point that we could overcome our reluctance to stage an uprising. So far, however, they have always been clever enough to relieve the pressure before it reached the breaking point. Thus far the pressure has not risen high enough to set off a liberating explosion." But the pressure continued to build throughout the German navy, and in 1917 the sailors mutinied. Another mutiny occurred in 1918, which led to the German revolution that same year (see sidebar).

Stumpf's intense patriotism had never left him, so he was horrified at his transformation into a mutineer by November 1918. "My God, why did we have to have such criminal conscienceless officers? It was they who deprived us of all our love for the Fatherland, our joy in our German existence and our pride in our incomparable institutions," he wrote. He closed his diary on November 24, 1918, with a sorrowful note: "My Fatherland, My dear Fatherland, what will happen to you now?"

For More Information

Books

Horn, Daniel. *The German Naval Mutinies of World War I.* New Brunswick, NJ: Rutgers University Press, 1969.

Horn, Daniel, ed. and trans. *War, Mutiny and Revolution in the German Navy: The World War I Diary of Seaman Richard Stumpf.* New Brunswick, NJ: Rutgers University Press, 1967.

Helen Thomas

July 11, 1877
Liverpool, England
April 12, 1967
Eastbury, England

Writer, memoirist

Helen Thomas was the wife of Edward Thomas (1878–1917), one of England's most prominent poets in the first decades of the twentieth century. She was emotionally devastated when he died in combat in April 1917, and she turned to writing to deal with her grief. Her two-volume autobiography, *As It Was* (1926) and *World Without End* (1931), describes their life together and offers a detailed portrait of what life was like on the British home front during World War I. In her memoir, Thomas did not use the real names of the people she described, but it was obvious that she was writing an intensely personal account of her life with Edward. In 1972, under the supervision of Thomas's daughter Myfanwy, an edition was issued with a key to the characters' names. Uplifted by the success of her books, Helen Thomas recovered from her depression. During World War II (1939–45), on her farm, she sheltered mothers and children who were evacuated from London during the German bombing. She died on April 12, 1967, fifty years and three days after the death of her husband in battle.

"It is a great trial to me to write to inform you that your husband was killed this morning. . . . He has been so much my support through this difficult—and to me, uncongenial —work, and he has been so wise and kind in the help he has given me."

—John Thorburn, in a letter to Helen Thomas dated April 9, 1917, relating the death of her husband, Edward Thomas, in battle; reprinted in Dictionary of Literary Biography.

From Wife to Widow

Helen Thomas was born as Helen Noble in Liverpool, England, on July 11, 1877. She was the youngest of four children of James Ashcroft Noble, a literary critic who wrote for the leading journals of the day. When Helen was five years old, she moved to London with her family, and a few years later they moved to Lancashire, in northwest England. She described herself in her memoirs as "a delicate child—prone to asthma and croup," but she enjoyed going to the theater and studying violin. When she was ten, the family moved back to London. Her first job was as a nursery governess for a European family living there. When Helen was eighteen, she and her girlfriends formed a literary research society whose practice was to visit authors and artists in their homes. It was on one of these visits that she met Edward Thomas. They were married in 1896 and had three children: a son, Philip Merfyn, and daughters Bronwen and Myfanwy.

Edward Thomas's first book, *The Woodland Life,* was published in 1897. After he and Helen were married, he had left Oxford University to pursue his writing career, even though it meant financial hardship for his wife and child. They moved to Wales, where Helen taught at Beadles, a progressive coeducational boarding school. Edward and Helen enjoyed life in the Welsh countryside and made the acquaintance of many poets and authors, including the American Robert Frost (1874–1963), who was visiting them in 1914 when World War I broke out. The following summer, Edward Thomas decided to enlist in the Artists' Rifles, a special air service regiment. He became a lieutenant and was transferred in 1916 to the Royal Artillery. It was during this period that he began to write his war poetry, but only a few poems were published before he was killed by shellfire at Arras, France, on April 9, 1917.

Capturing Life on the Home Front

Helen Thomas wrote in her autobiography that her husband's decision to enlist was not looked upon favorably by her colleagues at the Beadles school. She wrote, "When I told a leading member of the staff that Edward had enlisted, he said disapprovingly, 'That's the last thing I should have expected him to do.' How I hated him for that remark, and hated more

A Transatlantic Friendship: The Thomases and Robert Frost

When Britain went to war on August 4, 1914, Edward and Helen Thomas were spending a summer holiday with American poet Robert Frost and his wife, Elinor, in Herefordshire, where the two couples had rented adjoining farmhouses. Edward Thomas and Robert Frost had only recently met, but they quickly became close friends and had a significant influence on each other's careers.

At the time, Frost was unknown in his own country, and he had recently brought his family to England, where two of his poetry books, including his important collection *North of Boston,* were published by British publishers. Thomas wrote some favorable reviews of this collection, and these helped establish Frost's reputation both in England and the United States. Frost returned to America in 1915, but he served as an important mentor to Thomas during a crucial period between 1913 and 1915 when Thomas was depressed over his writing career and was thinking of divorcing Helen (Frost advised him not to do so).

Helen Thomas described her husband's friendship with Robert Frost in *World Without End,* though she did not use Frost's real name and disguised her husband as "David." She wrote, "Our friend was a poet. Between him and David a most wonderful friendship grew up. He believed in David and loved him, understanding, as no man had ever understood, his strange complex temperament. The influence of this man on David's intellectual life was profound."

Robert and Elinor Frost did not like the way Helen Thomas had described Edward in her memoirs, and the Frosts broke off friendly relations with her. In the 1950s, Helen tried to arrange a reconciliation, but it was unsuccessful.

the schoolmaster smugness from which it came." In another passage, she described Edward's dislike of military life: "[H]e hated it all—the stupidity, the injustice, the red tape, and the conditions of camp life. But he worked hard to perfect himself in the job he had undertaken, to become a proficient soldier, and it was with real pride that he brought home his first stripe for me to sew on his sleeve."

Helen Thomas's detailed narratives provide an invaluable view of life on the British home front during World War I. Her lyrical descriptions of life in the Welsh countryside during

These men sort sacks of potatoes as the country faces food shortages. Helen Thomas's writings captured the problems, such as food shortages, that people on the home front faced during the war. *Reproduced by permission of Hulton Getty/Archive Photos, Inc.*

this period are in stark contrast to the horrible scenes that were unfolding on the battlefields in France, just a few hundred miles away. Remembering when war broke out in 1914, she wrote that "no excitement disturbed the peace of that beautiful orchard country, with its wealth of choicest apples, pears and plums hanging red and golden and purple from the branches of innumerable fruit trees." Such descriptions symbolized the mood of the British people at the time; to them it seemed that the war was happening in a faraway place, and they did not think it would last a long time. Helen also wrote a moving account of her last glimpse of Edward as he left their village to join the army: "A thick mist hung everywhere, and there was no sound except, far away in the valley, a train shunting [moving on the tracks]. I stood at the gate watching him go; he turned back to wave until the mist and the hill hid him. I heard the old call coming up to me: 'Cooee!' he called. 'Cooee!' I answered, keeping my voice strong to call again. . . . I put my hands up to my mouth to make a trumpet, but no sound came. Panic seized me, and I ran through the mist and the snow to the top of the hill, and stood there a moment dumbly, with straining eyes and ears. There was nothing but the mist and the snow and the silence of death."

It was this kind of narrative, full of personal details, that made Thomas's writings so meaningful to British readers, who could identify with an author who had shared their own feelings during the war. By focusing on her feelings and not on political or diplomatic issues, Thomas endeared herself to the British public, who bought her books in great numbers during the 1930s.

Writing Her Way Out of Despair

Edward's death in April 1917 dealt a devastating emotional blow to Thomas. She described her initial grief in a journal entry as "these terrible days that so nearly were utter despair." It took her several years to get over her depression. Friends suggested that she try to put her feelings down on paper, and the result was two autobiographical volumes: *As It Was* and *World Without End*. *As It Was* was published in 1926 under the initials H. T., and *World Without End* was published in 1931. A combined edition of the two volumes was published in 1935 and reprinted in 1956 and 1972.

After her husband's death, Thomas tried to make a new life on Edward's small military pension. She rented a cottage at Otford but moved to London at the suggestion of her doctor, who thought she needed the company of friends and access to cultural attractions. With the success of her books, she recovered her emotional health and moved to a farm in the 1930s. For the last thirteen years of her life, she lived in a thatched cottage at Eastbury, on the banks of the river Lambourn. She died there on April 12, 1967.

For More Information

Books

"Helen Thomas." In *Dictionary of Literary Biography*. Vol. 216. Detroit, Mich.: Gale Group, 2000.

Thomas, Helen. *As It Was*. London: William Heinemann, 1926; New York and London: Harare, 1927.

Thomas, Helen. *World Without End*. London: William Heinemann, 1931.

Thomas, Helen, with Myfanwy Thomas. *Under Storm's Wing*. Manchester and New York: Carcanet Press, 1988.

Thomas, Myfanwy, ed. *Time and Again: Memoirs and Letters by Helen Thomas*. Manchester: Carcanet, 1978.

Web sites

Evans, William R. "Robert Frost and Helen Thomas: Five Revealing Letters." [Online] http://www.dartmouth.edu/~library/Library_Bulletin/Apr1990/LBA90Evans.html (accessed April 2001).

"Helen Thomas." *Encyclopedia of the First World War*. [Online] http://www.spartacus.schoolnet.co.uk/WthomasH.htm (accessed April 2001).

Wilhelm II

January 26, 1859
Berlin, Prussia (now Germany)
June 4, 1941
Doorn, The Netherlands

Kaiser (emperor) of Germany

For thirty years, from 1888 to 1918, Wilhelm II led Germany as its kaiser, or emperor, until he was forced to abdicate (resign from the throne) and go into exile after Germany's defeat in World War I. He went to the Netherlands and lived there in virtual isolation for twenty-three years He died in 1941, during World War II (1939–45), when the Netherlands was under German occupation. Wilhelm II was a grandson of Queen Victoria (1819–1901) of Great Britain and of Emperor Wilhelm I (1797–1888) of Prussia (the most powerful of the several German states that unified into the nation of Germany in 1871). Wilhelm II led Germany during its period of rapid modernization in the late nineteenth and early twentieth centuries. His ambitions to make Germany a major military and naval power and his sometimes reckless diplomatic maneuvering in Europe were primary factors leading to World War I, and they ultimately spelled disaster for him and his nation. John Van der Kiste's biography of Wilhelm II, published in 2001, suggests that some degree of mental instability, as well as personal animosities, fed Wilhelm's dislike for England and fueled his grand political strategies to dominate Europe.

"During his reign Wilhelm was spoken of indulgently as the man who wanted to be the bride at every wedding and the corpse at every funeral. One of the shrewdest judges of character of the time, his uncle King Edward VII called him 'the most brilliant failure in history.'"

—*From John Van der Kiste, Kaiser Wilhelm II: Germany's Last Emperor.*

Wilhelm II. *Reproduced by permission of Archive Photos, Inc.*

Early Life

Wilhelm II was born on January 26, 1859, in Berlin, the capital of Prussia, shortly before it became part of the larger German Empire that dominated much of Europe from 1871 through World War I. Wilhelm, of the Prussian royal house of Hohenzollern, was the eldest child of King Friedrich III and his wife, Victoria, daughter of Queen Victoria of Great Britain. Wilhelm had three brothers and four sisters. His full name was Friedrich Wilhelm Viktor Albert of Hohenzollern. Crown prince Wilhelm was born with a defective right arm that he later blamed on the ineptitude (lack of skill) of British doctors recommended by his royal grandmother. A mischievous and hyperactive child, Wilhelm was privately tutored from the age of seven by Georg Hinzpeter, a strict disciplinarian who subjected the young prince to a demanding regimen of study and physical exercise. Wilhelm studied philosophy and languages; he also played soccer and learned to sail and ride horseback. Hinzpeter encouraged Wilhelm to express himself, and he exposed the young man to a wide variety of common folk to prepare Wilhelm for his imperial duties later in life. Wilhelm spent holidays with his royal cousins at Windsor Castle in England and with his German cousins in Darmstadt.

In 1874, Wilhelm entered Bonn University to study political science and law, as well as literature, philosophy, and chemistry. Six years later, he became a captain and company commander of a military regiment. In 1881, he married Princess Augusta Victoria of Schleswig-Holstein-Sonderburg-Augustenburg, known familiarly as "Dona." They were married for forty years, until her death in 1921, and had seven children: six sons and one daughter.

Wilhelm's grandfather, the aged Wilhelm I, died in 1888. Wilhelm's father, King Friedrich III, was next in line for the throne, but he died after a reign of only ninety-nine days. Thus Wilhelm II succeeded to the throne within months of both his grandfather's and his father' deaths. Wilhelm II blamed his father's death, from cancer of the larynx, on the incompetence of British physicians, just as he had blamed an earlier generation of British doctors for his own defective arm. A ruler who exhibited anti-Jewish tendencies throughout his reign, Wilhelm also felt that British democracy (a government in which supreme power is held by the people) was too tolerant of liberal Jewish opinion. His personal dislike for the British, and his jealousy of their military and political power, would have an influence on Germany's diplomacy in the years to come.

Wilhelm as Kaiser (1888–1918)

The reign of Wilhelm II coincided with a period of modernization and industrial expansion in Germany. During the last two decades of the nineteenth century, Germany became the most powerful nation in continental Europe, largely through the influence of its powerful chancellor (head of state; similar to a British prime minister), Otto von Bismarck (1815–1898). The new kaiser and the old chancellor did not see eye to eye, however. One of their first clashes came during a coal miners' strike in the spring of 1889, when Wilhelm urged sympathy for the miners instead of the hardline (a strictly uncompromising course of action) advocated by von Bismarck. The kaiser and the chancellor soon found that they disagreed on many policies. Unwilling to share power with Bismarck, Wilhelm forced the chancellor to resign his post in 1890 and was succeeded by General Leo von Caprivi. In spite of his moderate social policies, Wilhelm believed strongly in the theory of the divine right of kings, which held that monarchs derived their right to rule directly from God, and he often upset his ministers and his grandmother, Queen Victoria, with aggressive statements that needlessly disturbed the balance of power in Europe. He allowed an important German-Russian mutual assistance treaty to lapse in 1890, which forced Russia to make an alliance with France three years later. Wilhelm also made it clear that he was interested in building up the German navy, which he thought essential to counterbalance Britain's domination of the high seas. These impulsive moves eventually forced Britain, France, and Russia into a closer alliance during the early 1900s, setting the stage for World War I.

When a crisis developed in the summer of 1914 after the assassination of Austrian archduke Franz Ferdinand in Sarajevo, Wilhelm failed to take the diplomatic steps that could have prevented the wider conflict. Historians believe that he could have convinced Austria-Hungary not to start the war with Serbia, or that he could have withheld full German

A World War I poster displayed in the United States to gain support for the war effort. The poster suggests that Kaiser Wilhelm be overthrown from power in Germany. *Reproduced by permission of Hulton Getty/Archive Photos, Inc.*

support and avoided drawing all of Europe into the war. But Wilhelm's pride kept him from looking out for the best interests of his country, and he moved toward war in order to save face. To build morale, he visited troops in the field from time to time (all six of his sons saw combat duty; the youngest, Joachim, was wounded in battle in East Prussia). However, Wilhelm disturbed his generals and German diplomats with his erratic moods and unrealistic expectations about how the war should be conducted. The kaiser often changed his mind on tactics and policy, causing his chief naval officer, Admiral Alfred von Tirpitz (1849–1930), to resign in frustration in the middle of the war. (Tirpitz was unable to convince the kaiser to allow Germany to engage in unrestricted submarine warfare; when Wilhelm finally agreed to that policy in 1917, it brought the United States into the war on the side of the Allies, effectively losing the war for Germany.) In general, Wilhelm clung to the belief that monarchies were superior to democracies; he thought that he and his royal cousins (King George V in Britain and Czar Nicholas II in Russia) would somehow work out a peaceful settlement, even though their nations were engaged in brutal conflict. When Nicholas was overthrown by the Russian Revolution in March 1917, Wilhelm was deeply distressed at the overthrow of his cousin and feared the effects that left-wing revolutionaries might have on his own empire.

Defeat and Exile

Wilhelm was forced to abdicate in November 1918, when the German chancellor signed an armistice (peace treaty) bringing World War I to an end. Wilhelm was given refuge at Doorn in the Netherlands, where he remained for the rest of his life. His wife, the deposed kaiserin (empress) Augusta Victoria, went into exile with him. She died in 1921, and the following

Kaiser Wilhelm II: Heir to a Prussian Tradition

Kaiser Wilhelm II's abdication in 1918 marked the end of the Hohenzollern dynasty, which had been a powerful force for some seven hundred years in the area now known as Germany. Always a powerful family, by the early 1400s, the Hohenzollern family took control of the state of Brandenburg, and in 1618 they added Prussia to their holdings. The first Hohenzollern to assume the title of King of Prussia was Friedrich I (1657–1713), who ruled from 1701 to 1713. His grandson, Friedrich II (1712–1786), was known as Frederick the Great; he ruled from 1740 to 1786. Frederick the Great increased the power and prestige of Prussia and added much new territory to his domain, including Silesia and part of Poland. He was considered an enlightened dictator because he read French and discussed some of the new liberal ideas circulating in Europe at the time. He also was a talented musician. At the same time, Frederick the Great helped establish Prussia's reputation for military power and discipline, strengths that were greatly admired by Wilhelm II a century and a half later.

Prussia, with its capital in Berlin, emerged as the most powerful state among a group of Germanic states. Otto von Bismarck (1815–1898) became chancellor of Prussia in 1862, and within a decade Prussia had won important victories in three wars, against Denmark (1864), Austria (1866), and France (1871).

Upon the defeat of France in 1871, many of the German states agreed to accept King Wilhelm of Prussia (1797–1888) as the first kaiser, or emperor, of a unified Germany. After his death, Wilhelm I was succeeded by his son, Friedrich III (1831–1888), who died after only ninety-nine days in power. Friedrich's son, Wilhelm II, then became Germany's third and last kaiser, from 1888 to 1918.

The militarism (the buildup of military power by governments) and expansionism (policy of enlarging a country by taking over other countries) that accompanied German unification during the last half of the nineteenth century helped set the stage for World War I. Under Wilhelm II, Germany came to see itself as the most important power in continental Europe. As heir to the Hohenzollern tradition, Wilhelm II advocated military discipline and steadfast devotion to duty. During the final months of World War I, when defeat seemed inevitable, he tried to boost morale of the German people by flatly stating that Hohenzollern family had never abdicated and would never abdicate. In 1940, when Wilhelm II was in exile in the Netherlands, he sent a congratulatory message to German Nazi leader Adolf Hitler after Germany occupied France, telling Hitler that this victory could be compared to the achievements of Frederick the Great and Wilhelm I, two of the great Hohenzollern rulers.

year Wilhelm married his second wife, Princess Hermine of SchönaichCarolath. In 1926, Wilhelm tried to rehabilitate his reputation by publishing a nostalgic memoir titled *My Early Life,* which described his life from childhood to the death of his father in 1888. The book downplayed strife and controversy, and Wilhelm chose to entirely ignore the period of his reign as kaiser and the events of World War I. Wilhelm wanted to erase his image as a tyrannical militarist, and his opening words in the book's preface show how he was trying to reinvent himself as a kindly old man: "In the loneliness of my exile in Holland [the Netherlands] my thoughts often travel back to the past. And the darker the present appears, the further these thoughts wander and seek the radiant sunshine of the happy years of peace and youth. Before my mind's eye the days return in which my Fatherland grew to unity and strength."

During World War II, as the German Nazi army spread across, Wilhelm remained at his estate in the Netherlands. Although he issued no diplomatic pronouncements, Wilhelm hoped that a new generation of Germans would achieve the victory that had eluded him a quarter-century earlier. Wilhelm died on his estate on June 4, 1941. Nazi Party leader and new German chancellor Adolf Hitler (1889–1945) wanted to give him a state funeral in Berlin. However, Wilhelm had requested that he be buried in Doorn if he died while still in exile, and that request was honored.

For More Information

Books

Clark, Christopher M. *Kaiser Wilhelm II.* New York: Longman, 2000.

Van der Kiste, John. *Kaiser Wilhelm II: Germany's Last Emperor.* Stroud, England: Sutton, 1999.

Wilhelm II. *My Early Life.* New York: George H. Doran, 1926. Reprint, New York: AMS Press, 1971.

Web sites

"Frederick Wilhelm Viktor Albert of Hohenzollern; Kaiser Wilhelm II of Germany." *Trenches on the Web.* [Online] http://www.worldwar1.com/biokais.htm (accessed March 2001).

"Kaiser Wilhelm II: A Place in the Sun." *Modern History Sourcebook.* [Online] http://www.fordham.edu/halsall/mod/1901kaiser.html (accessed March 2001).

Woodrow Wilson

December 28, 1856
Staunton, Virginia
February 3, 1924
Washington, D.C.

President, scholar, frustrated peacemaker

Woodrow Wilson, a scholar and university president who entered public life after a successful academic career, is regarded as one of the most influential presidents in U.S. history, largely because of his leadership during World War I and his earnest, though unsuccessful campaign to persuade the U.S. Senate to join the League of Nations, an international assembly that would encourage nations to resolve their disputes through peaceful means. A Democrat, Wilson served as the twenty-eighth president of the United States, from 1913 to 1921. In his first term, he was able to concentrate on his domestic "New Freedom" programs, which increased the power of the federal government to regulate business and the economy.

Wilson's second term was overshadowed by America's involvement in the Great War, later known as World War I. With Wilson as commander in chief, troops from the American Expeditionary Forces entered the war in 1917 on the side of the Allies (Great Britain, France, and Italy) and helped defeat the Central Powers (Germany, Austria-Hungary, and the Ottoman Empire). After an armistice (peace treaty) was

"I have seen fools resist Providence before, and I have seen their destruction, as will come upon these again, utter destruction and contempt. That we shall prevail is as sure as that God reigns."

—Woodrow Wilson, quoted in Arthur S. Link, ed., The Papers of Woodrow Wilson, *pp. 466–67.*

Woodrow Wilson.
Reproduced by permission of AP/Wide World Photos.

declared on November 11, 1918, Wilson traveled to the peace conference in Versailles, France, and presented his Fourteen Points plan for a new world order. This plan proposed the establishment of a League of Nations. But the American people had become strongly isolationist toward the end of the war; that is, many of them thought that America should keep out of European and other world problems. Because of this prevailing mood, Wilson was unable to convince the Senate to ratify U.S. participation in the League. In 1919, he embarked on a grueling nationwide tour to bring his case directly to the American people, but he suffered a paralyzing stroke and remained a virtual invalid for the remainder of his term. Despite this failure, Wilson is regarded as an early and serious internationalist (a person who believes in a policy of cooperation among nations for mutual benefit) who helped lay the groundwork for American participation in world affairs a generation later.

The Making of a Scholar

Thomas Woodrow Wilson—he dropped the first name in his adult years—was born on December 28, 1856, in Staunton, Virginia, the son of Joseph Ruggles Wilson, an Ohio-born Presbyterian minister, and Jessie Janet Woodrow Wilson, who had been born in England. The young Wilson was the third of four children. Soon after his birth, the Wilsons moved to Augusta, Georgia, where they were living when the Civil War broke out in 1861. Although he had been born in a northern state, Joseph Wilson sympathized with the Southern cause and served as a chaplain in the Confederate army. His son, the future president, witnessed horrible scenes of conflict, and it is likely that these memories stayed with him as he tried to negotiate a lasting peace after World War I.

In 1873, Thomas Woodrow Wilson entered Davidson College in North Carolina, but he had to withdraw the following year because of ill health. A year later, he entered the College of New Jersey (now Princeton University), where he participated in debate and public speaking and wrote for college publications before graduating in 1879. Later that year, he entered the University of Virginia Law School, and after graduation he began practicing law in Atlanta, Georgia. But Wilson loved the classroom more than the courtroom, and in 1885 he started teaching history and political science at Bryn Mawr College, a school for women near Philadelphia. The following year, he received his PhD in history from Johns Hopkins University in Baltimore, Maryland. In 1885, he wrote his first book, *Congressional Government,* which was widely praised for its analysis of the American political system. That same year, he married his first wife, Ellen Louise Axson; the couple eventually had three daughters. Ellen died in 1914, just after becoming First Lady. In 1915, Wilson married Edith Bolling Galt, who became a close advisor to her husband during the last two years of his second term, when he was a semi-invalid.

From the Classroom to the Political Arena

After teaching at Wesleyan University in Connecticut for two years, where he also coached the football team, Wilson joined the faculty of his alma mater, Princeton University, in 1890. There he taught jurisprudence (the study of law) and political economy. He remained a professor at Princeton for twelve years, during which time he wrote several more books, including his most important one, *A History of the American People,* published in 1902. That same year, he was elected president of Princeton University. Dressed in his familiar cap and gown, Wilson became a commanding presence on campus, taking bold steps to reorganize the college, improve its curriculum (courses of study), and make student life more democratic. His proactive approach was compared to the style used by Theodore Roosevelt (1858–1919), who was then president of the United States.

While at Princeton, Wilson also began to consider a political career. He accepted the Democratic Party's nomination to be governor of New Jersey and was elected to that office in 1910. As governor, he supported many progressive reforms, such as regulation of public utilities, workers' compensation, and antitrust legislation (laws designed to limit the power of "trusts," large corporations that work together to increase their power in the marketplace). Wilson's success as governor of this important state put him in the national spotlight. In 1912, the Democrats nominated Wilson as their presidential candidate. The national election was a three-way race: Running against Wilson were Republican William Howard Taft (1857–1930), the incumbent president (person already holding political office), and former president Theodore Roosevelt, the candidate of the Progressive, or Bull Moose, Party. Wilson easily won the election.

First Term as President (1913–17)

On March 4, 1913, Woodrow Wilson was inaugurated as the twenty-eighth president of the United States, with Thomas R. Marshall serving as his vice president. Wilson was often called "the schoolmaster in the White House" because of his career in education. During his first term, Wilson tried to implement what he called a "New Freedom" platform, which included antitrust legislation, a reduction of tariffs (duties, which are a kind of tax) on imported goods, and financial reforms. Among his successful projects during his first term were the Federal Reserve System, which is still in charge of U.S. banks, and the Federal Trade Commission.

When war broke out in Europe in the summer of 1914, Wilson tried to keep the United States "impartial in thought as well as in action." This was in keeping with a long American tradition of avoiding what George Washington once called "foreign entanglements." However, in accordance with the Monroe Doctrine, Wilson directed a foreign policy that took an active role in affairs in the Western Hemisphere, and he sent troops to Haiti and the Dominican Republic to protect U.S. interests there. The United States and Mexico nearly went to war in 1914 after Wilson sent U.S. forces to occupy Veracruz as a protest against Victoriano Huerta's military coup (sudden overthrow of the government) in Mexico City. After one Mexican faction, led by Francisco "Pancho" Villa (1878–1923), attacked the settlement of Columbus, New Mexico, in March 1916, Wilson sent General John Joseph Pershing (1860–1948) to lead a punitive expedition onto Mexican soil.

By this time, all of Europe was embroiled in the deadliest war to ravage that continent since the Hundred Years' War five centuries earlier. But Wilson continued to advocate U.S. neutrality despite growing German naval threats. When the *Lusitania,* a British ocean liner, was torpedoed by German submarines on May 7, 1915, more than a hundred Americans were killed, and there was much pressure on Wilson to enter the war against Germany. Wilson resisted the demands for outright war, but he strongly protested the German attacks on civilian vessels. He began a behind-the-scenes diplomatic campaign to assist the British and to prepare the United States for possible armed conflict. In the presidential election of 1916, Wilson's supporters used the slogan "He Kept Us Out of War" to persuade voters to reelect Wilson for a second term. During the campaign season, Wilson secured the passage of more progressive legislation, like aid to farmers, an eight-hour workday for railroad workers, a bill to end child labor, and higher income taxes on the rich. Wilson and Marshall won reelection over the Republican candidates, Charles Evans Hughes and his running mate, Charles W. Fairbanks. This time, however, the vote was much closer. The Wilson-Marshall ticket won 277 electoral votes, and the Hughes-Fairbanks ticket won 254—the closest electoral college margin until the election of 2000.

Second Term as President (1917–21)

Early in 1917, the Germans stepped up their U-boat (submarine) attacks on American vessels, and in April Wilson asked Congress to declare war "to make the world safe for democracy." On April 6, 1917, Congress voted overwhelmingly to enter the war, marking the first time in U.S. history that troops were sent to fight in Europe. Led by Pershing, who had earlier led the expedition in Mexico, the American Expeditionary Forces (AEF) soon arrived in France, helping relieve the weary Allied troops who had been fighting for three years. Under Wilson's leadership, the American people united to support the war. In May 1917, Congress passed a Selective Service act that required young men to be drafted into the armed services.

On January 8, 1918, Wilson gave his famous Fourteen Points address, in which he described his ideas for the postwar reconstruction of Europe on the principles of openness, democracy, and self-determination (the idea that countries should be able to determine their own political destinies without interference from other countries). Key to Wilson's plan was the establishment of a League of Nations, an international assembly that would encourage nations to resolve their disputes through peaceful means. In the Fourteen Points address, Wilson's humanitarian, idealistic side came through strongly: He wanted to persuade the Allies not to punish the Central Powers after the war; he hoped both sides would work together to achieve democracy and economic development in every coun-

British prime minister Lloyd George (left), French prime minister Georges Clemenceau (center), and U.S. president Woodrow Wilson at the Versailles peace conference in 1919. *Reproduced by permission of Archive Photos, Inc.*

try. Wilson's diplomacy helped persuade the Germans to accept the armistice of November 11, 1918. The armistice officially terminated what has been called "the war to end all wars."

At the end of November, Wilson sailed for the peace conference at Versailles, near Paris, France, becoming the first American president to visit Europe while in office. At the conference, he represented the United States as one of the "Big Four," the leaders of the victorious Allied powers, a group that

The United States Emerges as a World Power

Although the United States had gone to war with Great Britain in 1812, Mexico in 1846, and Spain in 1898, it maintained a steadfast policy of not committing troops outside the Western Hemisphere until 1917, when Woodrow Wilson dispatched the American Expeditionary Forces to Europe during World War I. The American people supported the troops "over there" in a burst of patriotic frenzy, but Wilson misread the mood of the country: Americans still favored George Washington's advice to steer clear of foreign entanglements.

During the nineteenth century, the United States was too busy expanding a new nation and fighting its own civil war to worry much about European affairs. By the early 1900s, though, things were changing, and the United States began to emerge as a world power in its own right, especially after World War I (1914–18) devastated Europe. During his term as president (1901–09), Theodore Roosevelt sent the U.S. Navy around the world to demonstrate American sea power, and he won the Nobel Peace Prize for his mediation in the Russo-Japanese War. Woodrow Wilson, too, won a Nobel Peace Prize, in 1919. Historians now believe that Wilson made some serious miscalculations in making his case for the League of Nations, especially by stubbornly refusing to include his political opponents in the peace negotiations.

Today, Wilson is widely considered to have been a thinker ahead of his time. His plan for a League of Nations was largely realized in 1945 with the creation of the United Nations, an international body that helps resolve disputes between nations. Ever since World War II (1939–45), America has been very involved in world affairs. It has fought wars in Korea, Vietnam, and Iraq, and it has participated in United Nations actions in Africa and the Balkans. Though critics complain that the United States has become the world's bully, imposing its will on smaller, less powerful countries, it seems likely that Wilson would have been pleased with America's role as a dominant player in promoting peace around the world.

included Prime Minister David Lloyd George (1863–1945) of Great Britain, Premier Georges Clemenceau (1841–1929) of France, and Prime Minister Vittorio Orlando (1860–1952) of Italy. Wilson was idolized by many Europeans for his principled stand and was awarded the Nobel Peace Prize for 1919. However, he was forced to compromise some of his positions in negotiations with his colleagues, who wanted to impose harsher penalties on Germany than what Wilson thought was desirable. Still, Wilson stubbornly refused to abandon his dream of international cooperation through the League of Nations. But when he returned to the United States in January 1919, he confronted strong opposition from the American public and Congress: They were glad to be out of the war and "foreign entanglements," and they wanted to concentrate on domestic matters. Because it was one of the terms of the peace treaty, membership in the League had to be approved by a two-thirds majority in the U.S. Senate. Wilson's chief Republican opponent in Congress, Senator Henry Cabot Lodge (1850–1924) of Massachusetts, became a bitter opponent of the League, but Wilson vowed to bring the question directly to the American people. He embarked on an eight-thousand-mile cross-country tour, speaking in city after city. Wilson emphasized the importance of international cooperation, and in reference to the treaty, he asked Americans, "Dare we break it and break the heart of the world?"

A Broken Champion of Peace

Wilson's own heart was broken as he came to realize that the mood of the American people was very much at odds with his vision. In September 1919, while speaking in Pueblo, Colorado, he nearly collapsed and had to return to Washington, D.C., where he suffered a stroke a week later. For the rest of his term, he remained in virtual seclusion in the White House. During this time, his wife, Edith Bolling Galt Wilson, is believed to have made important state decisions on his behalf. Without Wilson to fight for it, the Versailles treaty failed to make it through the Senate. Instead, the United States made a separate peace with Germany (outside the plan of the Paris Peace Conference) and never joined the League of Nations. In retrospect, some historians believe that U.S. membership in the League could have helped prevent the emergence of Nazism (a political movement led by Adolf Hitler that promoted racism and the expansion of state power) in Germany as well as the Second World War some twenty years later. Postwar America underwent its own difficulties: Racial and class conflict erupted into violence, and Wilson was unable to restrain his attorney general, A. Mitchell Palmer, from severely restricting civil liberties during the crisis. An example of such restrictions is the Eighteenth Amendment to the Constitution, which was ratified by the states in 1919. This amendment prohibited the manufacture, sale, or transportation of alcoholic beverages. However, in 1920, they also ratified the Nineteenth Amendment, which expanded individual liberties by giving women the right to vote.

Because of his health, Wilson was unable to run in the presidential elections of 1920, the first in which women were able to vote in all forty-eight states. The national ticket of Warren G. Harding and Calvin Coolidge easily defeated Democrats James M. Cox and Franklin D. Roosevelt (the latter had served as an assistant secretary of the navy in Wilson's war cabinet and would, like Coolidge, later serve as president of the United States). Wilson died in Washington, D.C., on February 3, 1924, and is buried in the National Cathedral there.

For More Information

Books

Heckscher, August. *Woodrow Wilson: A Biography.* New York: Scribner, 1991.

Knock, Thomas J. *To End All Wars: Woodrow Wilson and the Quest for a New World Order.* New York: Oxford University Press, 1992.

Link, Arthur S., ed. *The Papers of Woodrow Wilson.* Vol. 68. Princeton: Princeton University Press, 1993.

Osinski, Alice. *Woodrow Wilson: Twenty-Eighth President of the United States.* Chicago: Children's Press, 1989.

Randolph, Sallie G. *Woodrow Wilson, President.* New York: Walker, 1992.

Rogers, James T. *Woodrow Wilson: Visionary for Peace.* New York: Facts on File, 1997.

Walworth, Arthur. *Woodrow Wilson.* 3rd ed. New York: W. W. Norton, 1978.

Films

The American President (series). PBS, 2000.

Web sites

"Woodrow Wilson: A Brief Overview." *Woodrow Wilson House.* [Online] http://www.woodrowwilsonhouse.org (accessed April 2001).

Woodrow Wilson Birthplace. [Online] http://www.woodrowwilson.org (accessed April 2001).

Alvin C. York

December 13, 1887
Pall Mall, Tennessee
September 2, 1964
Nashville, Tennessee

Farmer, mountain man, humanitarian

"I didn't want to go and kill. I believed in my bible. And [it] distinctly said "THOU SHALT NOT KILL." And yet old Uncle Sam wanted me. And he said he wanted me most awfull [*sic*] bad. And I just didn't know what to do. I worried and worried. I couldn't think of anything else. My thoughts just wouldn't stay a hitched."

—*Alvin York, in David D. Lee,* Sergeant York: An American Hero.

Alvin C. York. *Reproduced by permission of AP/Wide World Photos, Inc.*

The story of Sergeant Alvin C. York embodies one of the great contradictions of war. If killing is wrong, how can society justify war? Further, how can nations convince good people to suspend the normal rules of civilization during wartime so that they can kill the enemy? A religious man who had sincerely tried to become a better person through devotion to his church, York had never been more than fifty miles from his home when he was sent to fight in France during World War I. Although he was a most unwilling soldier, York used the shooting skills he had developed in the mountains of Tennessee to become one of the most famous heroes of the war. However, York was not proud of his talent for killing, and he never wanted fame for it. He spent his life after the war trying to create some lasting good for the mountain people he loved.

A Hardscrabble Life

Alvin Cullum York was born on December 13, 1887, in a two-room cabin in the Wolf River valley in Tennessee's Cumberland Mountains, a region known for its poverty, isolation, and fiercely independent inhabitants. His parents, William

178

and Mary York, had eleven children and worked hard to make a living from the family farm. William York added to their income by working as a blacksmith. In this lean existence, hunting was not a sport but an important part of survival, and at a very young age little Alvin went out regularly with his father, learning the sharp shooting skills that would put meat on the dinner table. He learned how to kill a turkey with a single shot to the head, and he supplemented the family income by winning local turkey shoots and other contests.

Though he developed rifle skills and learned about farming the rocky mountain soil, York received very little schooling because he could not be spared long from his chores. For a few years he went to the tiny local school when he could, but he only got through third grade, attending classes for a total of nine months. York was never able to read well, and he regretted his lack of education. Giving other mountain children the chance to learn would become his mission when he was older.

The Taming of the Roughneck

In 1911, York's father died, leaving York with even more responsibility for taking care of the family. Along with farming and hunting to put food on the table, York earned a little money as a day laborer working with railroad or highway crews. It was at this time that York began to display many bad habits. He drank and gambled and spent his free time in rowdy bars, a combination of activities that often ended in fights.

After a few years of wild, drunken escapades, York found several reasons to change his life. He was at heart a serious man, and he knew that the rowdy life would lead him into trouble, perhaps jail or even death. His best friend, Everett Delk, was killed in a barroom fight, and York's mother was terribly worried that the same thing might happen to her son. Perhaps the most important factor in York's change of lifestyle was his growing attachment to a young neighbor woman, Gracie Williams.

York had never been much of a churchgoer, but Gracie took him to her church, the Church of Christ in Christian Union. York was "saved," that is, he had a spiritual experience in which he felt that God spoke to him, and in 1914 he became an active member of the church. The Church of Christ in Christian Union was a strict sect (a religious organization), for-

Conscientious Objectors: Those Who Refuse to Kill

As long as there have been wars, there have been those who think war is wrong and do not wish to participate. In modern times, these people have been called conscientious objectors (COs), meaning that their sense of what is morally right (conscience) forces them to object. COs have been treated with varying degrees of harshness at different times, but in the United States it has traditionally been assumed that someone whose religious or moral beliefs forbid fighting in a war should not have to fight. Sometimes COs are given a noncombat role in a war, such as driving an ambulance. Sometimes they are given some kind of work at home that supports the war effort, such as a job in a government office. Sometimes they are allowed to do work apart from the war that benefits society in some way, like charity work. However, COs are sometimes punished for not fighting. During the 1991 Persian Gulf War, more than thirty-five COs were put in jail for refusing to fight.

Though armies do not usually appreciate the moral strength of COs, it takes courage to refuse to fight when one's country demands it. Sometimes COs who were considered cowards and traitors during wartime are recognized later as heroes for standing up for their beliefs. One of these is Franz Jagerstatter, an Austrian farmer who refused to fight for the Nazis during World War II and was executed for his actions in 1943.

bidding drinking, dancing, movies, swimming, and swearing, and it was opposed to war or violence of any kind. By 1917, York was second elder, a high office in the church, and his roughneck life was behind him for good.

The Backwoods Hero

In 1917, the United States entered World War I, and York was drafted. He applied for conscientious objector status, which is sometimes granted to those whose religious convictions do not permit them to fight. But because York's church was small and not recognized nationally, his application was refused. Torn between his religious belief that war was wrong and his loyalty to his country, York left Tennessee on November 15 to report for duty at Camp Gordon, Georgia.

The officers who trained York were amazed by his skill with a rifle. Though he refused to practice by shooting at targets shaped like human beings, he could hit his mark at five hundred yards. He was assigned to a combat unit, Company G in the Three-hundred-twenty-eighth Infantry attached to the Eighty-second Division. York was still very hesitant about killing people in combat, however, and his commanding officers, Captain Edward Danforth and Major George Edward Buxton, worked hard to convince him that the war was a holy cause and that God was on the side of the Allies. On June 27, 1918, the Tennessee mountain man arrived in France.

The most famous moment of York's life came a few months later. On October 8, his platoon was ordered to capture a German machine-gun installation in the Argonne Forest in northern France. The American platoon sneaked up on the German troops; the Germans appeared to surrender, but then quickly signaled another group of German soldiers to open fire. Almost all of the Americans were killed. Left with only a handful of men, York used his rifle to pick off the German machine gunners, just the way he used to shoot turkeys through the head on his mountain hunting trips. When the Germans, infuriated, sent five men with bayonets to kill the American marksman, York calmly shot each of them, starting with the one in the back so that the men in front would not know what was happening—another turkey-hunting technique.

Stunned by the sudden defeat of their machine guns, the Germans surrendered their position. On the march back to the Allied lines, York gathered more prisoners for a total of 132. Almost singlehandedly, he had left 25 Germans dead and 35 machine guns disabled. He was promoted to sergeant and received many medals, including the French *Medaille Militaire* and Croix de Guerre, the Italian *Croce de Guerra,* and the American Medal of Honor. However, York was not happy about what he had done. The day after the battle, he took a small platoon back to search for survivors. At the site, he knelt and prayed for all the Americans and Germans who had died there.

Back to "Normal"
Back in the United States, the heroic adventure of York had captured the public imagination. The drama of the simple Tennessee mountain man who had defeated a regiment of Ger-

mans appealed to Americans who were sad and cynical about the war. On his return home in May 1919, York was overwhelmed by attention from the American press and public. But he was not proud of having killed during the war, and he did not want to be a public figure. He went home to the Wolf River valley and married Gracie Williams. He remained active in the Church of Christ in Christian Union, and in 1926 he founded the Alvin C. York Institute, a school for the young people in his home county of Fentress. To raise money for the school, he traveled around the country speaking about his experiences in the war.

In 1941, in spite of his church's ban on movies, York agreed to a film version of his life, starring the famous actor Gary Cooper (1901–1961) as York. The movie made York famous to a new generation and gained support for the nation's entry into World War II (1939–45). The film and his speaking engagements provided York with a good income, but he had never learned about handling money. He gave much of it away, made bad investments, and was often in debt; but his community and supporters around the country rallied many times to help him, Gracie, and their seven children. In 1954, York had a stroke and never fully recovered. He died in 1964 of another stroke, at the Nashville Veterans' Hospital, surrounded by his family.

The Alvin C. York Institute still exists as part of the Tennessee public school system. The success of this institute made York more proud than the fame he had won shooting his rifle in the Argonne Forest.

For More Information

Books

Lee, David D. *Sergeant York: An American Hero.* Lexington: The University Press of Kentucky, 1985.

Perry, John. *Sgt. York: His Life, Legend, and Legacy: The Remarkable Untold Story of Sergeant Alvin C. York.* Nashville, Tennessee: Broadman and Holman, 1997.

Skeyhill, Thomas John. *Sergeant York, Last of the Long Hunters.* Philadelphia, Penn., and Chicago: J. C. Winston, 1930.

York, Alvin Cullum. *Sergeant York, His Own Life Story and War Diary.* Ed. Tom Skeyhill. Garden City, NY: Doubleday, Doran, 1928.

Films

Sergeant York. Produced by Jesse L. Laksy and Hal B. Wallis and directed by Howard Hawks (Warner Brothers Pictures, 1941). Twentieth Century-Fox Video, 1982. Videocassette.

Web sites

"Alvin C. York." [Online] http://www.alvincyork.org (accessed May 2001).

"The Life of Alvin C. York." [Online] http://volweb.utk.edu/Schools/York/history.html (accessed May 2001).

Index

Bold type indicates main entries and their page numbers. Illustrations are marked by (ill.)

French Socialist Party 65
French, John 56–57
Freud, Sigmund 78
Friedrich I 167
Friedrich II (Frederick the Great) 167
Friedrich III 164, 167
Frost, Robert 113, 158–59
Fyodorovna, Alexandra 34–41, 34 (ill.), 37 (ill.)

G

Gallipoli 7
George V 166
Germany
    armistice signed by 103
    final offensive launched by 60, 102–03
    militarism and expansionist policy in 167
    modernization and industrialization in 163, 165
    revolution in 150–52, 154–55
Geronimo 119
Gestapo 74
Ghost Dance Rebellion 119
Goethe, Johann Wolfgang von 70
Gorky, Maksim 70
Graves, Robert 89, 112–13, 115
Great Depression, the 33

H

Habsburgs 43
Haig, Douglas 54–61, 54 (ill.), 57 (ill.)
Haldane, Richard 56
Hardaumont 130
Harding, Constanza 72
Harding, Warren G. 177
Hauptmann, Gerhart 70
Hawker, Lanoe 135
Herzl, Theodor 4
Hindenburg, Paul von 97, 100–04, 100 (ill.)
Hitler, Adolf
    as leader of Nazi Party 69, 83, 130
    condemned by George Creel 33
    Ludendorff's association with 104

Wilhelm II's association with 167–68
Hohenzollern 164, 167
Hollweg. *See* Bethmann Hollweg, Theobald von 101
Hoover, J. Edgar 82
Hôtel des Invalides 50
Hughes, Charles Evans 173
Humanitarian organizations, assistance of, during WWI 23
Humanitarians
    Cavell, Edith 19–26
    Kollwitz, Käthe 68–76
    York, Alvin C. 178–83
Husayn ibn 'Alī 87

I

Ibsen, Henrik 70
Imperial War Conference (1917) 16
Industrial Revolution 63
Islam 9, 11
Israel 1, 5

J

Jagerstatter, Franz 180
Jaurès, Jean 62–67, 62 (ill.), 66 (ill.)
Jewish people, homeland proposed for 4–5, 87
Jewish people, persecution of, in Europe 1–2, 4, 65, 75, 129
Joffre, Joseph 130

K

Kemal, Mustafa. *See* Atatürk, Mustafa Kemal
Kemalists 11
Kilmer, Joyce 147
Kingsley, Charles 63
Klinger, Max 70
Kollwitz, Käthe 68–76, 68 (ill.)
Kreisler, Fritz 32, 77–83, 77 (ill.), 80 (ill.)
Kurdish rebellion in Turkey 11

V

Vauban, Sébastien 50
Verdun, battle of 97, 128,
    130, 133
Versailles, Treaty of 52, 176
Victoria (queen of Great Britain)
    35–36, 38, 163
Villa, Francisco "Pancho"
    121–22, 172
Villain, Raoul 67
Vimy Ridge 15–16

W

Wadi Run 87
War bonds. *See* Liberty Bonds
War Council for the Red Cross 23
War poets 111–13, 147
War resistance movement in
    Belgium 22, 24–25
Westminster, Statute of (1931) 16
White Army, the 41, 93
Wilhelm I 163–64, 167
Wilhelm II 19, 71, 97, 99,
    100–01, **163–68**, 163 (ill.)
Wilson, Woodrow 23, 27, 29,
    169–77, 169 (ill.), 174 (ill.)
Women's roles during WWI
    Aaronsohn, Sarah 1–5
    Cavell, Edith 19–26
    Fyodorovna, Alexandra 34–41
    Kollwitz, Käthe 68–76

Mata Hari 105–10
    Thomas, Helen 113, 157–62
Women's status in Turkey 10
Women's voting rights in the
    United States 177
Works Progress Administration
    (WPA) 33
World War I, battlefield
    conditions during 116 (ill.)
World War I, beginnings of 42,
    165–66
WPA (Works Progress
    Administration) 33

Y

Yekaterinburg 40–41
YMCA assistance during WWI 23
York, Alvin C. 178–83, 178 (ill.)
    flim about, scence from
    182 (ill.)
Young Bosnians, the 46
Ypres, first battle of 52, 57
Yugoslavia 46

Z

Zangwill, Israel 4
Zelle, Margaretha Geertruida.
    See Mata Hari
Zionism 4
Zola, Émile 70